3RD EDITION

# TEXT TYPES
## A WRITING GUIDE FOR STUDENTS

ANNE **TOWNSEND** / ANNE **QUILL**

with ELLI **HOUSDEN**

T0359350

NELSON
A Cengage Company

Australia • Brazil • Mexico • Singapore • United Kingdom • United States

NELSON
A Cengage Company

Text Types: A Writing Guide for Students
3rd Edition
Anne Quill
Anne Townsend
with Elli Housden

Publisher: Alyssa Lanyon-Owen and Sam Bonwick
Project editor: Kathryn Coulehan
Editor: Nick Tapp
Proofreader: Julie Wicks
Cover design: Petrina Griffin
Text designer: Belinda Davis
Cover image: iStockphoto/MG_54
Permissions researcher: Wendy Duncan
Production controller: Christine Fotis
Typeset by: Q2A Media

Any URLs contained in this publication were checked for
currency during the production process. Note, however, that
the publisher cannot vouch for the ongoing currency of URLs.

Acknowledgements
The publisher would like to credit and acknowledge the
following sources for photographs and text extracts: p. 3
Shutterstock.com/El Nariz; p. 7 Alamy Stock Photo/Design Pics
Inc; p. 9 Alamy Stock Photo/PhotosIndia.com LLC; p. 35 text
extract adapted from http://www.swansea.ac.uk/media-
centre/news-
archive/2017/theonetrilliontonneiceberglarsenciceshelfriftfina
llybreaksthrough.php; p. 41 Shutterstock.com/kotoffei; p. 49
Getty Images/iStock/hidesy; p. 67 (top) Shutterstock.
com/ksuper, (bottom) Shutterstock.com/yskiii; p. 69 (top)
Shutterstock.com/sdecoret, (bottom) Getty
Images/iStock/CreativeImages.

For product information and technology assistance,
in Australia call **1300 790 853**;
in New Zealand call **0800 449 725**

For permission to use material from this text or product, please email
**aust.permissions@cengage.com**

National Library of Australia Cataloguing-in-Publication Data
A catalogue record for this book is available from the National Library of
Australia

Cengage Learning Australia
Level 7, 80 Dorcas Street
South Melbourne, Victoria Australia 3205

Cengage Learning New Zealand
Unit 4B Rosedale Office Park
331 Rosedale Road, Albany, North Shore 0632, NZ

For learning solutions, visit **cengage.com.au**

Printed in China by 1010 Printing International Limited.
7 8 9 10 26 25 24 23 22

# Introduction

*Text Types: A Writing Guide for Students,* 3rd edition, has been updated and expanded in the variety of text types and examples provided. Examples of more than 30 text types are analysed, including many electronic texts, and presented for the first time in full colour. There is a writing activities section at the back of the book so students can practise. Terms that appear in bold blue type are defined in the glossary.

This guide illustrates many of the elements of the major strands – Language, Literature and Literacy – underpinning the Australian Curriculum: English.

| LANGUAGE | <ul><li>text structure and organisation</li><li>expressing and developing ideas</li></ul> |
| --- | --- |
| LITERATURE | <ul><li>responding to literature</li><li>creating literature</li></ul> |
| LITERACY | <ul><li>texts in context</li><li>interacting with others</li><li>interpreting, analysing and evaluating</li><li>creating texts</li></ul> |

According to the Australian Curriculum, students in Years 7 to 10 are expected to plan, draft and publish imaginative, informative and persuasive texts using effective vocabulary and language features appropriate for the writer's purpose and the audience.

These texts may take a variety of formats, e.g. an everyday explanatory text, a media report, a literary text, a point of view or an argument expressed in a letter to the editor or a debate. *Text Types: A Writing Guide for Students,* 3rd edition, provides students with examples of all of these texts and more, together with clear directions about how to write each one. The book aims to provide the scaffolding and modelling necessary for the development of writing skills.

Most of the text types are presented in a double-page format, with one page analysing the structure of the text type and the second page presenting an example of the text.

The **structure** is analysed according to the following headings:
- Types – texts that fall into the category of each text type
- Context – the subject matter, the roles and relationships relevant to the writer and reader/s, the medium in which the writing is presented and the mode of presentation
- Language structures – the vocabulary and grammar appropriate to the task.

An example is included for each text type. Literary, factual texts and digital texts are represented in the guide.

*Text Types: A Writing Guide for Students,* 3rd edition, provides teachers, parents and students with a unique tool to improve writing skills and is suitable for use by students in mid-primary to mid-secondary school.

# Contents

## 1 Purpose

The purpose of an advertisement is to present a summary of information about a product or service in order to sell it to the public.

## 2 Types

- Online banners
- Posters
- Large-format billboards

## 3 Context

**Subject matter:** wide variety of subjects; can be serious, educational or entertaining and lighthearted
**Roles and relationships:** The author has the knowledge and tries to persuade the reader or viewer.
**Medium:** boards, paper, cardboard, online
**Mode:** written, drawn

## 4 Text

### How to prepare an advertisement

**Structure**

- Put the information into draft form, i.e. written, visual.
- Decide how the information will be organised, e.g. questions and answers; main heading and subheadings; blocks of information.
- Sequence the information.
- Decide how to record the information, e.g. writing, painting, drawing, computer-generated.
- Decide how to arrange the pictures, maps, labels; there may be more visuals than written text; use of bullet points.
- Apply appropriate font sizes:
  - title – largest font; should be readable from at least five metres away
  - subheadings – large
  - supporting material – medium
  - details – smallest.

**Vocabulary**

- list of attributes or features of the topic or subject
- persuasive or emotive
- text to suit the audience
- text to suit the product
- optional use of humour, rhyme

**Grammar**

- short sentences; complete sentences not always necessary
- phrases and single words – use of 'our' and 'you'
- adjectives and adverbs
- captions
- short headings
- present tense
- imperatives, e.g. *Try our NEW deluxe burger now!*

# NEED A
# Burger Boost?!

**LIMITED OFFER! ONLY $5.95**

**Try our NEW deluxe burger now! Freshly made with the finest ingredients**

A fresh beef patty flame-grilled just for you!
Served in a brioche bun, smothered in our secret deluxe
sauce with crisp lettuce, juicy tomatoes, crunchy onion,
tangy pickles and tasty cheese.

burgerboost.com.au 141 Newtown Rd, Bayview

## 1  Purpose

The purpose of a biography is to inform readers by retelling the events, experiences and achievements of a person's life.

## 2  Types

- **Biography:** an individual's life story written by another person
- **Autobiography:** an individual's life story written by himself/herself

## 3  Context

**Subject matter:** The focus is on the experiences and achievements of a person.
**Roles and relationships:** The writer states facts and is generally not known to readers.
**Medium:** book, magazine, encyclopaedia, Internet, radio, television, oral histories
**Mode:** written, spoken

## 4  Text

### How to write a biography

**Structure**

- Orientation: name the person, tell when and where he/she lived and state why he/she is famous.
- Series of events: list the important events in chronological order. Mention people or experiences that may have influenced his/her achievements. Explain the causes and effects of events.
- Reorientation: restate why the person is famous and say what contribution he/she has made to society.
- Visual content: include photographs, pictures or illustrations of the person and his/her achievements.

**Vocabulary**

- impersonal language for descriptions of events or achievements, i.e. do not use *I, we*
- descriptive but not exaggerated language, e.g. *Ned was always angry*
- emotive expressions, e.g. *he decided that the police picked on the poor*
- classifying language, i.e. put the person in the context of time, place and group, e.g. *His story has become a legend and Ned Kelly is the most written-about Australian.*
- time sequencing; explain events in a logical order in terms of time, e.g. *during the late 1800s*

**Grammar**

- verbs: active verbs rather than passive verbs, e.g. *There was a shootout with the gang that lasted for almost half a day.*
- verb form: past tense, e.g. *His fame grew*; present tense, e.g. *Ned Kelly is the most written-about ...*
- cause and effect language, e.g. *As a result*
- contrasting ideas or statements linked by appropriate connectives, e.g. *however, but*

# Ned Kelly

Ned Kelly was a famous highwayman who became a legend in Australia during the late 1800s. His fame grew because of his exploits as a bushranger and his fight for equality for the poor.

He was born in Victoria in 1854 to Irish parents. When Ned was 12 years old his father died. He had to leave school to become the breadwinner of the family so he worked for his grandfather and became involved in illegal work with horses and cattle. At the age of 14 Ned was jailed briefly for assaulting a Chinese immigrant. Also at this time it was thought that he had become involved with bushranger Harry Power but the police could never manage to prove a link.

In 1870, he spent another six months in prison for beating up a salesman and a year later was found guilty of being in possession of a stolen horse and served three years in Pentridge gaol.

Ned was always angry about what he thought was unfair treatment. He decided that the police picked on the poor so he and his relatives took their revenge on the local wealthy landowners by rustling their cattle.

One night, Kelly shot a policeman named Constable Alexander Fitzpatrick in the wrist because he didn't like the way the constable had treated his sister. Fitzpatrick swore he'd pay the Kelly family back and he made a false report about the incident, leading to Kelly's mother being jailed for three years. So Ned and his brother Dan, together with friends Steve Hart and Joe Byrne, went to live in the bush to avoid the police. They became known as the Kelly Gang. They robbed at least two banks, including a daring raid on the town of Jerilderie in New South Wales where they captured the town's policemen, locked them up and then took more than 2000 pounds from the bank's vault. At this time Ned Kelly wrote his famous Jerilderie letter, describing again how the police had treated his family and the poor so badly.

In 1879 the Kelly Gang's trademark armour was created to afford them better protection against police bullets. It was fastened together with iron bolts and held on with leather straps. It weighed about 44 kilograms and could stop a bullet. However, it was to prove ineffective for some of the gang in the final shootout.

On 26 June 1880, the Kelly Gang killed a former friend-turned-police informer, Aaron Skerritt. Then they returned to Glenrowan to prepare a trap for the police, who were travelling by train. When the police reached the township, there was a shootout with the gang that lasted for almost half a day. In the end, three of the Kelly Gang died, and Ned was severely wounded and easily captured. As a result, he was taken to Melbourne and later sentenced to death.

On 11 November 1880, 25-year-old Ned Kelly was hanged at the Old Melbourne Goal. This earned him the dubious distinction of being the first white, Victorian-born prisoner to be executed in Victoria.

His story has become a legend and Ned Kelly is the most written-about Australian.

Name

**Orientation:**
- Name
- Dates
- Reasons for fame

List of important events in his life

His quest for equal rights for the poor

Kelly Gang formed

Trademark armour created

Final days

**Reorientation**
- The legacy of Ned Kelly

## 1 Purpose

A blog or web log is a type of website or part of a website. It is usually set up by writers who make regular comments and may add descriptions, graphics or videos. It is written to inform, instruct, persuade or entertain.

## 2 Types

- **Commentaries** e.g. opinions on issues, current affairs
- **Reflections** e.g. on a movie or piece of music; diary; autobiography
- **Projects** e.g. a combination of text, images, links to other blogs or web pages
- **Art** e.g. photographs (photo blog), videos (video blogging), music (MP3 blog) and audio (podcasting)
- **Thematic tasks**
- **Journal writing** such as:
  - book reviews, weekly reviews
  - reflections on school events, excursions and camps; reflections on movies, music, books
  - reactions to school events or world events
  - feelings about a particular unit of work
  - individual portfolios
  - personal diary
- **Collaborative tasks** e.g. a book club that includes teacher and student posts, comments and discussion; class story
- **Research tasks** e.g. research findings outlined; data collected and published for analysis by the students

## 3 Context

**Subject matter:** variety of educational and non-educational subjects
**Roles and relationships:** The author contributes to a collaborative text, journals ideas or evaluates own progress; writes for known or unknown readers who may contribute to the text.
**Medium:** Internet, via computer
**Mode:** written, spoken

## 4 Text

Structure, grammar and vocabulary for the blog will depend on the blog's purpose and type, e.g. report, biography, personal diary, notes on self-evaluation.
**The following website will help construct a blog: http://edublogs.org/.**

# Nadia's book reviews

## Categories

FICTION     NONFICTION     RECOMMENDED

*Posted on 6 July 2018*
*Posted by Nadia*

**A Most Magical Girl** by Karen Foxlee

I loved this book! Annabel Grey is a great character and the author has created a very magical world in Victorian London. I review the book in full in the video below. SPOILER ALERT!

### POSTS

July 2018 (3)
June 2018 (5)
May 2018 (8)
April 2018 (4)
March 2018 (6)
February 2018 (1)
January 2018 (7)
December 2017 (2)
November 2017 (11)
October 2017 (6)
September 2017 (10)
August 2017 (22)

### TAGS

JK Rowling
Robyn Bavati
Fantasy
JRR Tolkien
Andy Griffiths
Picture books
Shaun Tan
John Marsden
Humour
Drama
Karen Foxlee
Bruce Pascoe

## 1 Purpose

The purpose of a brochure is to inform the public about the availability of goods and services.

## 2 Types

- Informing people about services available, e.g. government and health brochures; library services
- Advertising goods and services for sale, e.g. fun parks; shopping; travel
- Promoting events and activities, e.g. fetes; festivals; public meetings; sports events

## 3 Context

**Subject matter:** variety of subjects. The focus is on providing information to attract people to the activity or goods described.
**Roles and relationships:** The writer writes for unknown readers.
**Medium:** brochure = several joined pages; flyer/pamphlet = one page

## 4 Text

### How to write the text for a brochure/flyer

**Structure**

- title
- general introduction
- details outlined in paragraphs
- headings for paragraphs
- often, question and answer format, *e.g. What should I do if …*
- clear layout so it is easy to locate information, e.g. address, opening times, cost
- largest print for the most important ideas

**Vocabulary**

- language to appeal to the target group, e.g. if written for children, use simple, easy to understand language
- factual information and persuasive words and phrases
- focus on the participants or readers; language may appear quite personal and informal

**Grammar**

- verbs: action verbs; imperative (command) verbs, *e.g. Book now!*
- nouns: proper names with capitals, *e.g. Twenty20*
- use of short sentences, phrases, bullet points
- use of exclamation marks to convey excitement

# Twenty20

*Faster than test cricket!*

*More exciting than one-day cricket!*

## Yes, it's T20!

### WHY COME?

T20 cricket is a great night out for the whole family. It's 3 hours of entertaining, fast-paced action. The atmosphere is electric!

### RULES

There are two teams who bat for a single innings each of 20 overs. Their aim is to score as many runs as possible. The team who has bashed the most runs at the end of their 20 overs wins!

### ENTERTAINING

Non-stop entertainment from the start. Right through to the end, everyone in the family – from the youngest to the oldest – will be amazed at the action, music and fireworks. A great night out!

### THIS IS NOT A TEST!

Watch as each player hits the ball as far and as fast as they can. Will it be a six or will it be out? Every ball is a possibility.

### COST

T20 is a very affordable night out, with family tickets starting from $48. Book now!

### GETTING THERE

Your T20 ticket provides free public transport to the grounds.

### FACILITIES

As a world class facility, 'The Don' provides comfortable seats, all with great views of the action. A variety of food and drink options caters for all, from the good old meat pie, to more gourmet and healthier options. Or, bring your own food and un-opened drinks!

## 1 Purpose

The purpose of a debate is to put forward an argument in a formal structure to prove a case.

## 2 Types

- Class debates
- School and interschool competitions

## 3 Context

**Subject matter:** Both sides of an issue are presented for debate.
**Roles and relationships:** Teams of three speakers debate the topic.
**Medium:** in person; television; radio
**Mode:** spoken, with preparation in writing

## 4 Text

### How to write an argument for a debate

**Structure for preparation of a team's case**
- Read the topic.
- Brainstorm the topic.
- Record every idea that will support the team case, whether weak or strong.
- Build a case by choosing the ideas that most strongly prove the team case.
- Discuss each word in the topic so that all team members understand the topic; the first speaker in the debate must define the keywords in the topic.
- Focus on the single general reason why the topic is true or untrue.
- Discuss all the ideas in the team's case and decide which points each speaker will outline to prove his/her argument; make sure that each member of the team knows exactly what the other two speakers will be saying.

**Structure of arguments**
- introduction
- thesis (writer's opinion):
  - Present arguments with supporting evidence, i.e. make the point, elaborate and give examples.
  - Link ideas and paragraphs.
  - Make a recommendation that links directly to the position taken.
- conclusion: Revise thesis, present a summary of the points made.

**Vocabulary**
- use of appropriate language related to the issue
- may be biased, i.e. promoting one opinion but tries to look objective or logical in arguing this opinion
- well-chosen emotive words such as descriptive adjectives and adverbs, e.g. *exciting sport*
- focus on groups not individuals e.g. *students*
- use of persuasive language essential for maximum impact and participation
- use of hypotheses, e.g. *If this happens, then ...*

**Grammar**
- passive verbs may be used to convey opinions in an impersonal way, e.g. *is required*
- verbs indicating obligation are common, e.g. *must, need to, should*
- modal, i.e. verbs to limit the main verb (could, can, may, might, would etc.), e.g. *You may think ..., but I will convince you ...*

## 5  How a debate is judged

**Adjudicator**

Judges a debate. The adjudicator marks each member of the team and the combined marks of the three speakers are the team's overall result. Each speaker is judged on:

- matter
- method
- manner.

**Points for rebuttal**

- Try to attack the focus of the debate and the supporting proof.
- No direct personal remarks can be made; it is the arguments that should be attacked.
- Explain how and why the argument is wrong, e.g. *The opposition said ...*

## 6  Note-taking during a debate

Listen carefully and make notes on the following:

- keywords and terms defined by the opposition
- arguments made by the first and second speakers
- summaries made by the opposition
- rebuttal – a clear statement explaining how and why the speaker disagrees with the opposition's arguments.

## 7  Roles for speakers

| Speaker | Affirmative | Negative |
|---|---|---|
| **Speaker 1** | • defines keywords and terms<br>• outlines team's interpretation of the topic<br>• introduces team mates and gives a brief overview of their roles<br>• states affirmative case | • accepts or rejects the affirmative team's definitions, redefines if necessary<br>• accepts or rejects the affirmative team's interpretation, reinterprets if necessary<br>• introduces team mates and gives a brief overview of their roles<br>• rebuts case of the first affirmative speaker<br>• states negative case |
| **Speaker 2** | • rebuts the case argued by the first speaker for the negative<br>• states affirmative case; new arguments introduced | • rebuts the case argued by the second affirmative speaker<br>• states negative case; new arguments introduced |
| **Speaker 3** | • more impromptu than speakers 1 and 2<br>• rebuts second negative speaker<br>• states affirmative case; no new arguments introduced<br>• summarises the case for the affirmative | • more impromptu than speakers 1 and 2<br>• rebuts third affirmative<br>• states negative case; no new arguments introduced<br>• summarises the case for the negative |

## 8  Models for speakers

| Speaker | Affirmative | Negative |
| --- | --- | --- |
| **Speaker 1** | *Chairperson, fellow debaters and members of the audience. The topic we are debating today is …*<br><br>*We, the affirmative team, define the topic in this way …*<br>*and therefore we maintain that …*<br><br>*As the first speaker I will examine …*<br>*while our second speaker will demonstrate …*<br><br>*Our third speaker will sum up and conclude our team's argument.*<br><br>First speaker then:<br>• presents his/her argument and examples<br>• summarises points and presents a conclusion.<br><br>*We leave you in no doubt that …* | *Chairperson, fellow debaters and members of the audience. As the opposition has stated, the topic that we are debating today is …*<br>• There is no need to redefine the argument if you agree with the opposition's definition.<br><br>*The first speaker for the affirmative stated …*<br><br>*As the first speaker for the negative, I will examine …*<br>*while our second speaker will demonstrate …*<br><br>*Our third speaker will sum up and conclude our team's argument and the debate.*<br><br>First speaker then:<br>• presents his/her argument and examples<br>• summarises points and presents a conclusion.<br><br>*We leave you in no doubt that …* |
| **Speaker 2** | *Chairperson, fellow debaters and members of the audience. The first speaker of the negative said …*<br><br>*However, we maintain that …*<br><br>*The first speaker for the affirmative has told you that …*<br>*and I, as second speaker, will argue that …*<br><br>Second speaker then:<br>• presents his/her argument and examples<br>• summarises points and gives a conclusion. | *Chairperson, fellow debaters and members of the audience. The first speaker of the opposition said …*<br><br>*However, we maintain that …*<br><br>*The second speaker of the opposition said that …*<br><br>*The first speaker for the negative has told you that …*<br>*and I, as second speaker, will argue that …*<br><br>Second speaker then:<br>• presents his/her argument and examples<br>• summarises points and gives a conclusion. |
| **Speaker 3** | • rebuts, summarises and concludes the case<br>• no new points are introduced | • rebuts, summarises and concludes the case<br>• no new points are introduced |

# 1st speaker [negative]

Good evening, chairperson, fellow debaters and members of the audience. As the opposition has stated, the topic we are debating today is: 'That skateboard riding is not an acceptable activity for inclusion in the school sporting program'.

Accepts or rejects the affirmative's definitions

As the first speaker for the negative team, I will examine the following ideas:
1   the importance of physical fitness
2   the development of skills through competition.

Our second speaker will outline the following points:
3   the importance of variety in a school sporting program to encourage maximum participation
4   the necessity of providing an alternative to team sports.

Our third speaker will sum up and conclude our team's argument.

Introduces team mates and gives a brief overview of their roles

I would like to point out some flaws in the opposition's argument. The first speaker for the affirmative said that skateboard riding is a dangerous sport. However, we maintain that, provided that the sport is carefully supervised and that the participants wear safety gear, accidents should be kept to a minimum.

Rebuts case of the first affirmative speaker

In a nutshell, schools need to recognise that skateboarding is a sport and should be included in the school sporting program. Skateboard riding requires a high level of fitness and develops skills that are necessary in other school sports such as soccer and cricket. *[Overview of case]*

First, physical fitness needs to be recognised as an essential part of this sport. In order to perform a variety of flips and turns, it is very important to have a high level of physical fitness. The school should encourage students to participate in a school fitness program designed to enhance balance, timing and agility that would benefit all sports, not just skateboarding. Cricketers would be advantaged by improvements in balance and timing and football players would appreciate the opportunity to improve all three skills. *[Argument 1]*

States the negative case

My second argument maintains that experience of competition is a requirement for the development of sporting ability. Skateboard riders enjoy the thrill of competition and the opportunity to improve their own performances. Students are able to choose from a variety of competitions. The sport is a non-contact sport and safety gear has to be worn at all times to protect students from injuries. *[Argument 2]*

To conclude, schools need to lift their bans on this exciting sport and allow kids to have fun. This sport provides opportunities for fitness, skill development and experience in competitions. Skateboard riding should be on the list of regular school sports from which students can make their choice. *[Summary – conclusion]*

## 1 Purpose

The purpose of a description is to inform using a factual or imaginative text. The focus is to describe, with accuracy and sufficient depth, the particular characteristics of specific people, animals, events and processes.

## 2 Types

- Descriptive paragraph, e.g. describing a character in a novel
- Descriptive chapter in a nonfiction book, e.g. the Inuit as an example of an ethnic group

## 3 Context

**Subject matter:** the characteristics and significance of specific people, places, animals, events and processes
**Roles and relationships:** The writer knows the facts/topic/character etc. and writes for known or unknown readers.
**Medium:** textbooks, encyclopaedias, novels, Internet, lectures, documentaries
**Mode:** written, spoken

## 4 Text

### How to write a factual description

**Structure**
- often written in reply to a question and so the sequence depends on the question
- initial sentence: a classification of the topic, e.g. name of plant, animal, river etc.
- subtopics: written in order of the question
- paragraphing: one paragraph per broad heading, e.g. species, habitat, risks to survival
- illustrations: photographs, diagrams or maps

**Vocabulary**
- adjectives and adverbs used to increase effectiveness of descriptions
- impersonal language, e.g. do not use I or we; do not give personal opinions

**Grammar**
- simple present tense verbs to describe people, places etc., e.g. *volcanic ash blocks rivers*
- present (and present perfect) tense, passive verbs to describe habitual events, e.g. *energy is harnessed*
- active verbs to describe actions done by people or animals, **e.g. *people return to their farms***

### How to write an imaginative description

**Structure**
- may be much more unstructured than a factual description

**Vocabulary**
- evocative language, e.g. adjectives and adverbs to provide colour; effective imagery to create word pictures
- may be personal or impersonal

**Grammar**
- flexible, varied, less formal, use of active and passive voice

# Description: factual

**Icelandic volcanoes**

Iceland has many active volcanoes because of its unique location on the mid-Atlantic ridge. The island has 30 active volcanic systems, 13 of which **have erupted** since the settlement of Iceland.

When volcanoes erupt, molten lava flows from them. Gases and ash are also spewed into the atmosphere. The ash that rises from volcanoes is very fine and can float for many hundreds of kilometres. Throughout their history, the people of the Icelandic region **have been severely affected** by volcanic ash and gases. On many occasions, their lives and communities **have been devastated**. People **have been forced** to move to other areas to escape the danger of poisonous gases.

Volcanic ash blocks rivers, destroys fishing sites and causes flooding. Consequently, the economy is seriously affected because fish and fish products are a major export item. In addition, volcanic eruption causes destruction of crops and livestock in a country where agriculture is a major occupation. If flooding occurs, roads and bridges are wiped out and communication is severely affected. Human and natural landscapes can be destroyed or changed forever.

······ Simple present tense verbs to describe people, places etc.

The high level of heat and activity inside the Earth, close to the volcano, can provide opportunities for generating geothermal energy. When this energy is harnessed, it is of significant benefit to the community. The use of geothermal heat **has been** one of Iceland's most valuable power sources for more than 60 years.

······ Present (and present perfect) tense, passive verbs to describe habitual events

The lava and ash that is deposited during an eruption breaks down to provide valuable nutrients producing very fertile soil in the long term. After these eruptions many people return to their farms to take advantage of this rich soil.

······ Active verbs to describe actions done by people or animals

# Description: imaginative

**The Fender**

The old Fender guitar sits in the corner waiting for its owner to return. Dust gathers on the stained brown cover. Inside, a bright red strap lies ready to be attached. Tied to the handles are two tattered airline tags from journeys made in another time. The cream guitar within lies waiting, longing for fingers to pluck at its strings again. At the top of the long neck, where each string is hooked through the eye of a silver tuning key, knobs are ready to be turned to tighten them, to restore their tune. They stretch down the slender neck of light brown wood snuggling into the off-white body of the instrument. The wood is slightly chipped along the edges and the broken volume knob indicates the many turns of the past. Frets are worn from the constant use of fingers pressing chords and picking notes. 'Stratocaster Made in the USA' is still displayed proudly on the top.

······ First sentence introduces the topic.

Word pictures with adjectives: *stained brown cover, tattered airline tags, slender neck of light brown wood*

Descriptive verbs: *snuggling, displayed, stained*

It longs to be used. Where are the fingers to make those strings come alive again?

## 1 Purpose

The purpose of email is to retell or comment on events, send greetings, provide information, e.g. to apply for a job.

## 2 Types

- Personal
- Social
- Business

## 3 Context

**Subject matter:** greetings, retelling events, conversations, gathering and giving information, job applications
**Roles and relationships:** The writer and the readers may be known or unknown to each other.
**Medium:** computer
**Mode:** written

## 4 Text

### How to write the email

**Structure**
- Information in boxes at the top of the message must be completed or the message will not be sent.
- Message requires:
  - email address of sender
  - email address of receiver
  - copies to others if appropriate
  - subject of the message.
- Begins with a salutation:
  - *Dear* [formal]
  - *Hello/Hi* [informal]
- Concludes by signing off:
  - *Yours sincerely, Tom Brown* [formal]
  - *Bye for now, Tom* [informal]
- Attachments, e.g. text or photos, can be included.
- Hyperlinks to the Internet can be included.

**Vocabulary**
- formal: the language of a letter, i.e. no slang, informal expressions or abbreviations
- informal: casual language, slang, abbreviations very common

**Grammar**
- personal pronouns: e.g. *I, we*
- formal: correct grammar; full sentences
- informal: grammar may be incorrect; phrases, rather than whole sentences, may be used; exclamation marks to convey emotion

# Formal

From: jjones@anisp.net.au
To: clarkc@abc.company.org
Subject: Application for the position of Sous Chef
Attached: Resume

Dear Mr Clark

I am writing in response to the advertisement posted on Seek.com for a Sous Chef at Martin's Restaurant.

Please accept my attached resume and letter in application for this position.

My skills and experience match the advertised position very closely and I look forward to hearing from you soon.

Yours sincerely
Jennifer Jones

# Informal

From: jjones@anisp.net.au
To: bill@myisp.com
Cc: fred@myisp.com; phil@anisp.net.au
Subject: Party tonight
Attached: Picture of team

Hi all

Bill's got into rugby for school! ... let's party ... my place ... 8.30pm tonight ... cya ...

Joe

## 1  Purpose

The purpose of an essay is to analyse a topic and present arguments to persuade an audience to one point of view.

## 2  Types

- TV debate or panel discussion
- Newspaper editorial
- Response to an assignment/examination task

## 3  Context

**Subject matter:** a current or controversial issue for discussion
**Roles and relationships:** The writer, as the authority, writes for unknown readers.
**Medium:** newspapers, magazines, debates, speeches, radio and TV current affairs programs
**Mode:** written, spoken

## 4  Text

### How to write an expository text

**Structure**
- introduction
- thesis (writer's opinion) – usually topic sentences introducing each paragraph
- format: arguments with supporting evidence/compare and contrast/cause and effect
- conclusion: thesis revised, summary of points made

**Vocabulary**
- formal, clear and persuasive language
- well-chosen emotive words, e.g. *stressed parents*
- focus on groups not individuals, e.g. *students*

**Grammar**
- use of present tense to describe current issues
- use of the verb 'to be', e.g. *is, are*
- use of verbs to describe mental processes, e.g. *think, believe*
- use of causal conjunctions, e.g. *If they have homework, then ...*; *due to*
- use of words to tie arguments together, e.g. *first, finally, in conclusion, to sum up*
- modality, e.g. *lots of, can/may/should, many, often, probably, possibly*

# Homework

**The amount of homework given to students needs to be reduced for several reasons.** In short, time is limited in many students' lives. At the same time, some students are showing alarming levels of obesity due to sedentary lifestyles. Finally, family disharmony has increased as a result of stressed parents trying to get their children to do their homework.

**Introduction**
- Thesis – writer's opinion

**First, time is limited.** Many students don't arrive home until 6 pm. This is because they have chosen to play sports which require a few hours of training each week or they engage in cultural activities, which are often taught after school. When they arrive home, they have to unpack their bags, do assigned chores, have a shower and eat dinner. By the time they have finished these necessities, it is 8 pm. If they have homework, then it is too late to start, and whatever is done may be of poor quality because they are tired. Therefore, it can be argued that there is not enough time after school to complete quality homework.

**First argument with supporting evidence**
- Topic sentence

**Added to this, many other young people are recording high levels of obesity because of their sedentary lifestyles.** Traditional homework is not an activity that is known to raise the heart rate and so does nothing to improve physical fitness. We are constantly being told to become healthier. Why sit still at night time when students have been sitting still in the classroom all day? This is not good for their health and contributes to the high levels of obesity seen today.

**Second argument with supporting evidence**
- Topic sentence

**Finally, homework places huge amounts of stress on already stressed-out families.** In many families both parents are working and the last thing they need is to fight with their children at the end of a stressful day. By reducing the amount of nightly homework, the family home would be a much more relaxed place, as it should be.

**Third argument with supporting evidence**
- Topic sentence

**Conversely, many parents and teachers argue that homework is a necessary part of daily learning but is it really necessary?** Surely being active for some parts of the day is also essential for students' wellbeing. Furthermore, some people may argue that homework develops discipline and good study habits for later in life. Yet, if students aren't ready or even mature enough to realise the benefits of such discipline, then homework becomes a negative, not a positive force.

**Paragraph to address possible rebuttals**
- Topic sentence

**Linking connectives**

**In conclusion, homework should be reduced.** We must recognise that students' time is limited, sedentary work contributes to the high levels of obesity among Australia's youth and finally, homework can cause an increase in family disharmony. The wellbeing of students is far more important than excessive amounts of homework.

**Conclusion**
- Recap of thesis

## 1  Purpose

An editorial presents the opinion of a publication on an issue. It can be used to persuade the reader to a point of view or present an opinion for analysis by the readers.

## 2  Types

Editorials can appear in a variety of publications, particularly newspapers, but also magazines and newsletters.

## 3  Context

**Subject matter:**
- World news – war, natural disasters, major catastrophes
- Local news – federal, state and local politics
- Social events – important visitors
- Sporting events – local, national, international

**Roles and relationships:** The writer presents the publication's view to a wide and unknown audience.

**Medium:** newspaper, magazine, newsletters

**Mode:** written

## 4  Text

### How to write an editorial

**Structure**
- introduction – presenting the publication's point of view
- background information
- principles of a basic argument:
  - introduction
  - paragraphs that elaborate on the issue – one reason for each paragraph
  - facts that support opinion
  - strong statement, either to link to the next sentence or paragraph, or to conclude

**Vocabulary**
- language that can be persuasive or emotive

**Grammar**
- use of simple and complex sentences
- longer paragraphs
- third person point of view

# Recreational drones

············ Headline

New legislation needs to be considered for
domestic use of unmanned drones to ensure
airspace safety and protect privacy.

Commercial aircraft and remotely controlled drone aircraft operated
by businesses may need to share the same airspace. Questions are
being asked about drone aircraft delivering pizza to consumers across
suburbs. Will they be flying in regular commercial airspace? There
is the issue of young people flying light drone aircraft between city
buildings or at dangerously low levels down a suburban street. Cars
moving along a street would have difficulty seeing them at this level
so there is need to consider the safety aspects of this activity.

Individuals are becoming concerned about neighbours using
domestic drones to hover next to their windows or in their backyards
to spy on them. In addition, there is a concern that law-enforcement
agencies may use drones to spy on the public with security cameras
in the sky.

Drone technology has become part of everyday life. It is important to
know that pilots of commercial drones weighing 2 kg or more need
to be registered with the Civil Aviation Safety Authority (CASA)
and have an operator's certificate before their UAVs (unmanned aerial
vehicles) go through public airspace.

However, there is the question of how existing privacy laws apply
to recreational drones. CASA advises it has plans to review the
recreational regulations and have new ones in place by the end of the
decade. It is clear unmanned aircraft technology and its capability is
changing fast and regulators need to develop new safety standards and
regulations in order to balance the requirements for safe operations
without impacting on its growth and potential.

This indeed will be a huge challenge.

**Stating the issues:**
- Unmanned domestic drones
- Sharing airspace
- Children flying drones
- Neighbours with drones

**Factual evidence**

**Opinion:** Challenge of balancing safe operations and growth of the unmanned sector

## 1 Purpose

The purpose of an explanation is to outline how, and/or why events occur; how things work or tasks are done.

## 2 Types

- Reports, e.g. historical, procedural
- Articles, e.g. magazines, newspapers, encyclopaedias

## 3 Context

**Subject matter:** The focus is on natural occurrences, historical and political events; objects such as machines; tasks or behaviours, e.g. how to play a game.
**Roles and relationships:** The writer is the authority; readers are being educated.
**Medium:** textbooks and encyclopaedias; newspapers and magazines such as science and sports magazines; Internet; response to examination/assignment task; TV programs
**Mode:** written; spoken from written text

## 4 Text

### How to write an explanation

**Structure**
- general statement about topic
- explanation or description of the stages/steps in the process in a logical sequence
- diagrams often support explanation

**Vocabulary**
- unbiased, exact language
- impersonal language
- 'time' words to indicate stages of the event, e.g. *first, finally*
- adverbs: descriptive words to indicate how something occurred, e.g. *most popular sports, 11 players each*
- adjectives: descriptive words to explain the process, e.g. *specialist players, new batting side*

**Grammar**
- simple present tense, e.g. *is*; simple past, e.g. *was*
- passive verbs, e.g. *First the coin is tossed.*
- action verbs, e.g. *One side fields and the other side bats.*

# How to play cricket

The game of cricket is one of the most popular sports played in Australia today. It is enjoyed by young and old, male and female, in cities and rural areas.

General statement about topic

Cricket is played by two teams of 11 players each. The aim of the game is for one team to bowl out the other before they reach the first team's run total. Each side usually bats and bowls twice. Each session is called an 'innings'. To start the game, a coin is tossed by the umpire and one captain will call 'heads' or 'tails'. Of course, only one can win this toss, so the captain who wins can choose to bat or field first.

Explanation or description of the stages/steps in the process in logical sequence

One side fields first, while the other team bats. The batting side tries to score as many runs as possible. Different shots earn different numbers of runs. For example, if a player hits the ball over the fence without it touching the ground on its way out, this is called a 'six', and six runs are awarded to that player.

Simple present tense, e.g. *fields*, *bats*

There are many ways of getting 'out', including being caught on the full or allowing the stumps (behind the batter) to be knocked over. Not every player in the fielding team will bowl. This position is reserved for specialist players, for example, a 'leg-spinner' or a 'pace' bowler.

Unbiased, exact language

Finally, when all players in the batting side are out, the fielding side becomes the batting side and vice versa. The new batting side will try to get more runs than the other side before being bowled out. The new fielding side will try to bowl out the batting side or 'take wickets' before they reach the run total.

## 1 Purpose

The purpose of an information report is to provide facts and details about a specific topic after careful study and investigation into the area. Maps, diagrams and tables may be used to illustrate findings.

## 2 Types

- Formal report
- Review
- Scientific report

## 3 Context

**Subject matter:** wide variety, e.g. natural and physical world; human environments
**Roles and relationships:** The writer is an authority and may be unknown to the reader.
**Medium:** Internet, books, encyclopaedias, historical, geographical and scientific texts, TV programs
**Mode:** written – including illustrations; spoken – may include a PowerPoint presentation with headings and key terms

## 4 Text

### How to write the information report

**Structure**

- opening statement: introduces the topic and provides information about location, classification or category
- purpose: states clearly the purpose of the report
- series of paragraphs: formal and clear organisation of information in paragraphs. Each paragraph begins with a topic sentence about a feature or aspect of the area of study. The body of the paragraph provides more detail about the topic introduced in the topic sentence. Habits, behaviours or uses are explained; objects may be classified.
- conclusion: sums up what has been discussed in the report
- diagrams, photographs, illustrations, tables and maps may be used to enhance the text
- bibliography: list of sources used to research the report

**Vocabulary**

- focus is on groups/categories, *e.g. dogs* rather than *my dog*
- related to subject
- technical terms commonly used

**Grammar**

- present tense is usually used, *e.g. are found, occurs*
- verbs 'to be' and 'to have' are common, *e.g. is, were, have, had*
- passive verbs, *e.g. were planted*
- cause and effect connectives used, *e.g. because, so, as a result of*
- modality – *can, would, should*

# Enoggera Creek

Title

The headwaters of Enoggera Creek are in the D'Aguilar Ranges near Mt Nebo. The creek flows down between the ranges and through many suburbs on its journey to the sea.

Opening statement

This report aims to determine the health of the creek and the effect of the introduction of non-native flora, domestic run-off and pollution.

Purpose

Many specimens of native flora and fauna have disappeared from the creek area. Trees have been cut down and this has reduced the number of animals that can live in the area because of the lack of protection or food sources. When we compare present photos with those of the past, we see that the previous diversity of plant and animal life no longer exists. Local residents have used the banks for disposal of garden clippings, and introduced species of plants have taken over the native flora.

**Features**
- *Report on the present condition of the creek by use of digital photos. Comment on the presence of flora and fauna.*

Water tests that have been carried out have shown that there is now a high level of toxicity in the creek. There are many factories along the banks and their waste products may be leaching into the water. This has reduced the numbers of native fish that can be sustained in the creek.

**Features**
- *Report on tests carried out on the water, life in the creek and plant growth.*

Often waste products and rubbish are found in the creek. This situation can cause injury or death to animals and fish if they become tangled in plastic bags or metal cans.

**Description of evidence today**
- *What flows into the creek? What is the result?*

Our findings would suggest that there is significant evidence of pollution in the creek. One solution would be to lobby council to impose more penalties on organisations that allow waste products to leach into the creek. As well, local residents should be made more aware of the problems caused by the disposal of their garden rubbish and should be urged to support clean-up days.

**Summary**
- *Report on the health of the creek from writer's findings and studies and suggest a solution to the problem.*

**Table of pollutants, Enoggera Creek**

| Type of pollutant found | | Number found |
|---|---|---|
| **Pollutants** | Plastic bags | 378 |
| | Glass bottles | 12 |
| | Metal cans | 44 |
| **Weeds** | Species A | 19 |
| | Species B | 60 |

Include map, diagrams, table of findings for water tests

# Reference list

Carter, J 2005, *Enoggera Creek: a case study*, Brisbane City Council, viewed 21 June 2010, http://www.ourbrisbane.com.au.

Kemp, L 2006, 'Water quality in Brisbane', *The Environmental Review*, Vol. 3, no. 6, pp. 19–23.

Reference list

## 1 Purpose

The purpose of an infographic is to summarise a variety of information onto one page. This page will include text and images, including graphs, to describe a concept in a way that can be easily understood.

## 2 Types

- Presentations
- Projects
- Explanations

## 3 Context

**Subject matter:** variety of factual/educational subjects
**Roles and relationships:** The author is the authority who presents a variety of information that can be clearly understood by the reader.
**Medium:** There are many online programs used to create an Infographic, e.g. Canva.
**Mode:** written

## 4 Text

### How to prepare an infographic

**Structure**

- Decide on the main message to get across.
- Preparation: research the content and sequence the information.
- Decide on the subheadings.
- Match the researched content with the subheadings.
- Decide on a theme.
- Decide on a colour scheme.
- Create your infographic. Make it appealing by using proportion and magnitude.
- Edit as necessary.

**Vocabulary**

- relevant and catchy
- can include bullet points or short sentences

**Grammar**

- short phrases
- single words

# KEY FACTORS CONTRIBUTING TO GLOBALISATION

## TRANSPORTATION OF PERISHABLE FOODS

### COLD-CHAIN TECHNOLOGIES

### REFRIGERATION

## DEVELOPMENT OF MULTINATIONAL CORPORATIONS

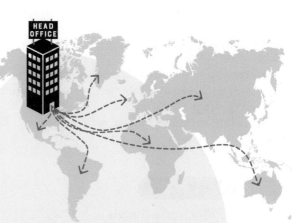

HEAD OFFICE

## IMPROVED COMMUNICATIONS

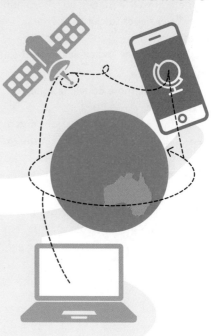

## REDUCTION IN TARIFFS AND OTHER BARRIERS TO TRADE

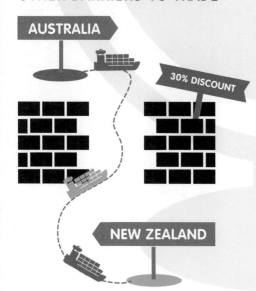

AUSTRALIA

30% DISCOUNT

NEW ZEALAND

## 1 Purpose

The purpose of an interview is to gather information from and/or about a person.

## 2 Types

- Personal and political interviews for private or educational research or for publication in the media, i.e. radio, television, magazines and newspapers, Internet
- Survey

## 3 Context

**Subject matter:** questions to a person about a particular subject
**Roles and relationships:** The interviewer is being educated by the interviewee, who is the authority and has the knowledge on the subject.
**Medium:** face to face; telephone; radio; television
**Mode:** spoken from a written text

## 4 Text

### How to conduct an interview

**Structure**
- Introduce yourself and state your background and purpose.
- Ask a variety of well-designed questions about the subject; some questions will be spontaneous as the interviewer needs to clarify answers.
- Review the answers with the interviewee.
- Thank the interviewee and explain how the answers will be used.

**Vocabulary**
- usually less formal, more conversational
- related to subject
- questions: start with simple questions and move on to more complex questions
- ask open-ended questions which gain the maximum amount of useful information, i.e. ask who, what, where, when and why questions
- limit closed questions requiring a yes/no answer, e.g. *Would you like to be famous?*

**Grammar**
- questions may require the past, present or future tense
- interviewer speaks in the second person, e.g. *you* and *your*
- interviewee speaks in the first person, e.g. *I, me, my*

# Interview

Hello, my name is …

Today we are interviewing adults from culturally diverse backgrounds who were born overseas. Our questions will be about the people and places that you remember from the past. The aim of this research is to …

**Places**

1  Can you describe the house in which you lived when you were a child?
2  Can you describe the room in which you slept as a child?
3  Can you describe the houses in the neighbourhood?
4  Where was your favourite place to visit when you were a child?
5  Where did you go when you wanted to hide?
6  Where did you go to school?
7  Describe the classrooms.
8  Where did you go to shop for food and clothes?
9  Describe your favourite places for fun and recreation.
10  What were your first impressions of Australia?

**People**

1  Who lived in your house with you as a child?
2  Can you describe your father or mother as you remember them from that time?
3  Who visited your house when you were young?
4  Tell me about your relatives, e.g. grandparents, aunts and uncles.
5  Who were your favourite cousins?
6  Who was the best cook in the family?
7  Describe someone in the family who had unusual characteristics.
8  Tell me about your neighbours.
9  Who were your favourite or most disliked teachers? Why?
10  When did your family decide to come to Australia? Why did they decide to come here?
11  Who were the smartest, richest, kindest or most religious people at that time?

Questions

Review

Thank you for taking the time to participate in this interview. The results of all interviews will be collated and incorporated into our research on the topic, *Cultural Diversity in Australia*.

Explain

## 1 Purpose

The purpose is to state a point of view, justify it and try to influence the reader's views; may be a strong complaint about an issue.

## 2 Types

- Letter to the editor of a newspaper, television or radio station

## 3 Context

**Subject matter:** controversial issues in the community
**Roles and relationships:** The writer is writing to an editor of a newspaper and unknown readers.
**Medium:** newspapers, magazines, television or radio station
**Mode:** written

## 4 Text

### How to write a persuasive letter to the editor
**Structure**
- date
- the address of the writer
- the editor's name/title
- name and address of the newspaper
- salutation: *Dear ...*
- purpose of the letter
- thesis: state your point of view
- arguments: state your arguments to support your point of view
- conclusions: restate your argument and recommend a solution
- sign off

**Vocabulary**
- personal language, **e.g.** *I urge you*
- emotive expressions, **e.g.** *thoughtlessness and ignorance*

**Grammar**
- tense: present tense to express an opinion about current issues
- cause and effect structures: *due to, because of, as a result*

23 February 2018 ·········································································· Date

14 Brown St
The Gap QLD 4061 ································································· Address

The Editor
The Courier Mail
41 Campbell St
Bowen Hills QLD 4006 ·················· Title, name and address
of newspaper

Dear Sir or Madam ······································································ Salutation

It has come to my attention that the local council has decided to
remove an area of natural bush in Main Street, The Gap, and allow
the land to be developed for housing. When we bought our house in ······ State your position
this area, the council assured us that this area would remain a natural
bush environment. We feel betrayed by such thoughtlessness and
ignorance.

This area is a favourite spot for local families to have leisurely Sunday
afternoon picnics. As it is beside a running creek, it provides a cool ······ Argument 1
and relaxing environment for everyone.

The creek area is special, because it has a platypus habitat that is
rarely found in metropolitan areas today. If this area is open to ······ Argument 2
development, these shy native animals will disappear forever.

Native birds are seen in abundance in the trees and a family of owls
returns each year to raise their chicks. This enables children to get to ······ Argument 3
know and appreciate our native wildlife.

I urge you, and your readers who live in this wonderful place, to take
action to prevent this housing development by voicing their opinions ······ Recommendation
at the council meeting next week before it is too late!

Yours sincerely ············································································· Signing off
James Brown

## 1 Purpose

The purpose of a narrative is to entertain.

## 2 Types

- Stories
- Myths
- Fables

## 3 Context

**Subject matter:** events, characters, issues or themes, e.g. a story about the relationship between a boy and his family

**Roles and relationships:** The writer may or may not know the reader of his/her story.

**Medium:** magazine, book, response to examination/assignment task

**Mode:** written

## 4 Text

### How to write the story

**Structure**

- orientation: introduction
- complication: a problem that needs to be solved, e.g. how to access the caves
- resolution: problem is solved
- sequence of events must be clear

**Vocabulary**

- may be a personal point of view, **e.g. *I*, *we***
- emotive, **e.g. *the two adventurers were desperate***
- descriptive, **e.g. *slippery brown walls***

**Grammar**

- action verbs, **e.g. *explore, crawled, escape***
- usually written in the past tense, **e.g. *checked, swam***
- direct speech is often used, **e.g. *Luke cried, 'The tide has closed our only exit!'***
- first or third person used
- use of time phrases to sequence events, **e.g. *when the tide came in ...***

# Survival

·········· Title

**Deep in the cave, with the water levels rising rapidly, the two adventurers were desperate to find an exit. There seemed little hope of escape.**

······ Introduce the story (optional)

Luke had often been to the beach with his family. He had wanted to explore the caves but people warned him that the entrance would close up when the tide came in. There was only a brief opportunity at low tide.

······ Orientation

The boys had already made plans to explore the caves, what they would need to take and what time of the day would be the best. Finally they arrived at the beach. They went out to explore the area around the caves and look for entrances either by sea or land. They checked tide times and estimated the perfect time to enter.

Rising early the following morning, they waited anxiously for low tide. They headed for the beach. The entrance was quite narrow but inside the cave was wider. Their head lights were reflected on the slippery brown walls as they crawled in. Luke led them along a narrow corridor that eventually opened into a large cavern with water dripping continuously from the ceiling into a clear underground lake.

They swam in the cool waters and found large and small sea animals that must have been peculiar to a place without natural light. Their colours were quite bland and you could see through their skin. It was a world of natural wonder.

They became too engrossed to notice how far they had swum into the cave and that the water level had begun to rise.

Suddenly Luke cried, 'The tide has closed our only exit!'

There seemed little hope of escape the way they had come in. They began searching for another way out. On the other side of the lake, two dark steep tunnels led upwards out of the cave. They needed to make a choice immediately. Which tunnel was an exit?

······ Complications

The one on the left looked easier. As they moved towards it, their head lights began to fade. To conserve battery power, Luke took the lead and Harry turned off his light. The pitch dark consumed them except for the light from Luke's helmet. They crawled onwards and upwards. Their thoughts strayed to questions of survival.

'What'll we do if it's a dead end?' said Harry in a panicky voice. They could not go back; the tide would have filled the cave by now. With Luke's light fading, the boys realised that they had come to another flat area. In front of them was a natural staircase in the rock wall. Peering through the darkness they saw a glimmer of light at the top. They climbed the stairs and found a large rusty metal cover at the top.

'Push, push!' Luke shouted urgently.

Struggling together, they managed to lift it up. Fresh air filled their lungs. They were safe ... this time!

·········· Resolution

## 1 Purpose

The purpose of a news article is to inform its readers of the latest news.

## 2 Types

- Factual account of a recent dramatic happening
- Social report
- Sports reports
- Current issues

## 3 Context

**Subject matter:**
- breaking world news, e.g. war, natural disasters, major catastrophes
- local news, e.g. newsworthy happenings on a federal, state or local level
- social events, e.g. important visitors, celebrities, weddings, funerals
- sporting events, e.g. local, national and international results and match summaries

**Roles and relationships:** The writer expects a wide and unknown audience of mature readers.

**Medium:** newspapers, magazines, Internet, radio and TV

**Mode:** written with captioned pictures, spoken (read from a written script)

## 4 Text

### How to write a report

**Structure**
- headline: immediate focus on the subject of the report
- byline: the reporter is named
- the lead: a short paragraph explaining what, where and when in relation to the news event
- important detail: comment by a witness or an observer
- consequences: further developments arising from the event
- text: written in columns and in short paragraphs
- paragraphing: items in the report, arranged in paragraphs in order of importance, like an upside-down triangle

**Vocabulary**
- usually objective language, without bias
- related to what happened: time, place and people involved

**Grammar**
- verbs: action verbs, **e.g. _has broken, calved_**
- verb form: past tense is used except for direct speech.
- passive verb form is common, **e.g. _that has warmed quickly in recent decades_**
- headline: present tense or passive verb form; may be a phrase without a verb; often a play on words, **e.g. _Iceberg away!_**
- direct speech for witnesses or observers

# Iceberg away! ·········································· Headline

*Martin Jones* ······································· Byline

One of the biggest icebergs on record has broken away from
Antarctica, creating an extra hazard for ships around the continent
as it breaks up. During the Antarctic winter scientists monitored the
progress of the splitting ice shelf using the European Space Agency
satellites. ······· Lead

The 1-trillion-tonne iceberg, measuring 5800 square kilometres,
calved away from the Larsen C ice shelf in Antarctica sometime
between July 10 and 12. 'It is one of the largest recorded and its
future progress is difficult to predict,' said Adrian Luckman, professor
at Swansea University and lead investigator of Project MIDAS, which
has been monitoring the ice shelf for years. 'It may remain in one
piece but is more likely to break into fragments. Some of the ice
could remain in the area for decades, while parts of the iceberg may
drift north into warmer waters,' he added. The iceberg, which is
likely to be named A68, was already floating before it broke away so
there is no immediate impact on sea level. The Larsen C ice shelf has
been reduced in area by more than 12 per cent. ······ Summary of the information

The Larsen A and B ice shelves, which were situated further north
on the Antarctic Peninsula, collapsed in 1995 and 2002, respectively.
'This resulted in the dramatic acceleration of the glaciers behind
them, with larger volumes of ice entering the ocean and contributing
to sea-level rise,' said David Vaughan, glaciologist and director of
science at British Antarctic Survey. 'If Larsen C now starts to retreat
significantly and eventually collapses, then we will see another
contribution to sea level rise,' he added. ······ Details

Big icebergs break off in Antarctica naturally so scientists are not
linking the rift to manmade climate change. However, the ice is a
part of the Antarctic Peninsula that has warmed quickly in recent
decades. Now it may add risk to the area, which is not on major trade
routes but it is the main destination for cruise ships visiting from
South America. Scientists seem to think that in the years and months
ahead the ice shelf could regrow, or be subject to further calving,
which may lead to a total collapse. ······ Consequences

Opinions are divided in the scientific community. The models
say it will be less stable, but any future collapse could be years or
decades away.

## 1 Purpose

To entertain

## 2 Types

Genre-based, e.g. adventure, classic, crime, fantasy, science fiction, young adult (YA)

## 3 Context

**Subject matter:** fictional story
**Roles and relationships:** writer to unknown audience
**Medium:** book format, audio book, e-book
**Mode:** written

## 4 Text

How to write a novel

**Structure**

- plot usually comprises: orientation, complication, series of crises, resolution
- divided into chapters
- characters: main character/hero/heroine and other subsidiary characters
- setting: usually creates a definite place, time and social setting, **e.g. *she had been born in India***

**Language**

- description of places, people, events, **e.g. *One frightfully hot morning***
- dialogue between characters, **e.g. *Send my Ayah to me.***
- action through the author or narrator's eyes, **e.g. *It was true, too.***
- vocabulary may be formal, colloquial, figurative, **e.g. *she was as tyrannical and selfish a little pig ...***

**Grammar**

- story may be told in first, second or third person, **e.g. *She had a little thin face***
- past or present tense, **e.g. *When Mary Lennox was sent to Misselthwaite Manor***

# Excerpt from *The Secret Garden*

## Frances Hodgson Burnett

When Mary Lennox was sent to Misselthwaite Manor to live with her uncle everybody said she was the most disagreeable-looking child ever seen. It was true, too. She had a little thin face and a little thin body, thin light hair and a sour expression. Her hair was yellow, and her face was yellow because she had been born in India and had always been ill in one way or another. Her father had held a position under the English Government and had always been busy and ill himself, and her mother had been a great beauty who cared only to go to parties and amuse herself with gay people. She had not wanted a little girl at all, and when Mary was born she handed her over to the care of an Ayah, who was made to understand that if she wished to please the Mem Sahib she must keep the child out of sight as much as possible.

So, when she was a sickly, fretful, ugly little baby she was kept out of the way, and when she became a sickly, fretful, toddling thing she was kept out of the way also. She never remembered seeing familiarly anything but the dark faces of her Ayah and the other native servants, and as they always obeyed her and gave her her own way in everything, because the Mem Sahib would be angry if she was disturbed by her crying, by the time she was six years old she was as tyrannical and selfish a little pig as ever lived.

The young English governess who came to teach her to read and write disliked her so much that she gave up her place in three months, and when other governesses came to try to fill it they always went away in a shorter time than the first one. So, if Mary had not chosen to really want to know how to read books she would never have learned her letters at all.

One frightfully hot morning, when she was about nine years old, she awakened feeling very cross, and she became crosser still when she saw that the servant who stood by her bedside was not her Ayah. 'Why did you come?' she said to the strange woman. 'I will not let you stay. Send my Ayah to me.' The woman looked frightened, but she only stammered that the Ayah could not come and when Mary threw herself into a passion and beat and kicked her, she looked only more frightened and repeated that it was not possible for the Ayah to come to Missie Sahib.

Detailed description of the central character

Use of adjectives and examples to establish personality

Reveals relationships with other characters

Dialogue creates insight into character

## 1  Purpose

An essay on a novel demonstrates knowledge of, and insight into, a literary text.

## 2  Types

- Academic text on an aspect of a novel
- Can be comparative, responding to two texts

## 3  Context

**Subject matter:** critical analysis of textual features of a novel
**Roles and relationships:** The writer is often a student, writing for an examiner or in an exam situation.
**Medium:** written literary criticism
**Mode:** written

## 4  Text

### How to write the novel essay

**Structure**

- introduction: names title and author and responds to the topic with a hypothesis
- body: develops the hypothesis in a series of sequenced paragraphs, e.g. issues introduced in the extract
- conclusion: restates the hypothesis and sums up the argument with a final evaluative comment, e.g. *Overall ...*
- paragraph structure uses topic sentences, e.g. *The focus of* The Secret Garden *is character development.*
- the body of the paragraph is an explanation providing evidence from the novel

**Vocabulary**

- formal language
- literary terms, e.g. *coming of age novel*
- linking words, e.g. *Another factor*
- conclusive words, e.g. *By the end of the novel*

**Grammar**

- complex sentences
- paragraph structure
- quotations from the text, e.g. *had not wanted a little girl at all ...*
- third person, e.g. *Initially, Mary ...*
- present tense, e.g. *There are several factors ...*

# Essay question: Discuss the central character in a novel you have studied and show how they develop in the text.

*The Secret Garden* (1911) by Frances Hodgson Burnett is an early coming of age novel. Set first in India, and then in England, it traces the development of the central character, Mary Lennox, from an unloved but spoilt child to a person who learns humility and selflessness from new companions in a new environment.

Introduction names title and author and states hypothesis

The focus of *The Secret Garden* is character development. At the outset of the story, Mary is an unattractive character. Despite her shortcomings, the reader is likely to feel sorry for this unloved child. Her mother 'had not wanted a little girl at all, and when Mary was born she handed her over to the care of an Ayah'. Initially neglected by her parents, Mary finds herself transported to England to live in the house of an absentee uncle she has never met.

Quotes from the novel provide evidence to support the hypothesis

There are several factors that lead to Mary's character development in the novel. The first is the new people that surround her, the staff of Misselthwaite Manor. Initially, Mary treats the servants with arrogance, just as she treated her ayah in India. However, she soon responds to their kindness. And when the maid, Martha, introduces her to Dickon, a wise boy of her own age, Mary makes her first friend.

Topic sentence signposts the topic of the paragraph and maintains relevance

Another factor in Mary's transformation is linked to nature and the new landscape in which she lives. Misselthwaite Manor is situated on the edge of the moors and Mary comes to love its wild beauty. But not as much as she loves the secret garden that she discovers behind a high wall on the estate. Beautifying the garden with her new friends becomes Mary's favourite activity. The garden holds a sad secret that Mary discovers at the end of the novel. Yet the ending is positive as the garden, once neglected like Mary, is now loved and cultivated with flowers and fragrant bushes.

Linking words are used for cohesion between paragraphs

Use of complex sentences

By the end of the novel, Mary is transformed into a healthy, likeable person. In *The Secret Garden*, Frances Hodgson Burnett has shown how life can be tragic, but that negative events can be overcome by human interaction and the forces of nature.

Conclusion restates the hypothesis and sums up the essay

## 1 Purpose

A podcast is similar to a radio show that is recorded and then distributed over the Internet, so that the audience can choose when to listen. Podcasting provides opportunities for students to share their work and experiences with a potentially huge audience.

## 2 Types

- Interview writing, e.g. students interview other students about their hobbies; students pretend to be somebody famous, such as a football star or television actor.
- Students write stories in groups on a theme.
- Outside broadcast [Science] – using an MP3 player with recording facilities, record a feature on location, e.g. around the school or on a school field trip. Download this to your computer and add it to your show.
- Jingles – use software such as Audacity (PC) or GarageBand (Mac) to create jingles. These can bring interesting features to a show.
- Add podsafe music.
- Use sophisticated software – e.g. MixCast Live (PC) is specifically designed for podcasters.
- Use a combination of iTunes and Nicecast for school podcasts.

## 3 Context

**Subject matter:** variety of educational and non-educational subjects
**Roles and relationships:** The writer should find out the intended audience so the podcast can be tailored appropriately.
**Medium:** Internet
**Mode:** written and spoken

## 4 Benefits

- Students learn to develop literacy skills, e.g. writing scripts, setting up interviews.
- Students learn to develop and practise their speaking and listening skills.
- Students learn new ICT skills.
- Can be interactive; the audience can be invited to send their comments.
- Develops teamwork
- Develops organisational skills, independent learning and responsibility

## 5 Setting up

The basic equipment needed is a computer with some kind of recording ability (an internal or external microphone) and some recording software. Audacity software is free and allows you to record your show and then export it as an MP3 file. You can then upload this to your school website, with permission. A school podcast can be a single recorded story that is put onto the school's social media page.

# Popular podcasts

1 Science Friday

2 Story Corps

3 This I Believe: Podcast

4 Youth Radio Podcast

5 60-Second Health

6 Classic Poetry Aloud

7 Grammar Girl Quick and Dirty Tips

8 Hubblecast HD

9 Stuff You Missed in History Class

10 HowStuffWorks NOW

## 1  Purpose

The purpose of poetry is to allow the writer to express personal and sensory impressions for the enjoyment of the reader.

## 2  Types

- Cinquain
- Haiku
- Limerick

## 3  Context

**Subject matter:** personal choice
**Roles and relationships:** written for readers known or unknown to the writer
**Medium:** books, magazines, Internet, personal diary, poetry readings
**Mode:** written, spoken

## 4  Text

### How to write a cinquain

**Structure**

- 1st line – title, names the participant – one word
- 2nd line – discusses the title – two words
- 3rd line – action words related to the title – three words
- 4th line – feelings related to the title – four words
- 5th line – synonym for the title – one word

**Vocabulary**

- The words focus on the name of the poem, the descriptions and the actions.

**Grammar**

- adjectives – *soft*, *gentle*
- verbs ending in 'ing' – *caring, listening, laughing*

### How to write a haiku

**Structure**

- no title
- 1st line – five syllables
- 2nd line – seven syllables
- 3rd line – five syllables
- traditional haiku has nature as the subject, modern haiku is more flexible

**Vocabulary**

- focuses on participant, relates to the subject

**Grammar**

- three lines
- adjectives and verbs; must fit in with syllable patterns

### How to write a limerick

**Structure**

- 1st line – who [the participant]
- 2nd line – about the participant/topic
- 3rd and 4th line – more details about the idea
- 5th line – restate the first line with some of the words or phrases changed which sums up the events from line 1

**Vocabulary**

- words focus on the people in the poems and their actions
- sequence of events
- humour

**Grammar**

- adjectives
- Lines 1, 2 and 5 match in rhyme and number of syllables.
- Lines 3 and 4 are shorter and rhyme.

# Cinquain

## Example 1

**Lorikeets**
Loud, larrikins
Flying, swooping, raucous
Coloured wings beat fast
Excitement

## Example 2

**Baby**
Crying, restless
Mother's arms encircling
Protective warm loving contented
Infant

**Pattern**

Line 1: Title

Line 2: Two descriptive words

Line 3: Description related to
the title

Line 4: Feeling related to
the title

Line 5: One word; may be
synonym for title

# Haiku

## Example 1

(This haiku is about eagles.)

Using wind currents
Majestically gliding
Freely moving … WOW

## Example 2

(This haiku is about crows.)

All so shiny, black
Observers from on high
Free to scavenge now

**Pattern**

No title

Five syllables

Seven syllables

Five syllables

# Limerick

There was an old lady from France
Who wanted to learn how to dance
But her feet felt so tired
After she tried and she tried
Oh the poor dear old lady from France

**Pattern**

Line 1: The participant

Line 2: Describes the participant.

Lines 1 and 2: Rhyme and have
the same number of syllables

Lines 3 and 4: The story is
developed; shorter rhyming lines

Line 5: Sums up the previous
events and repeats some
words from Line 1

## 1 Purpose

The purpose of poetry is to allow the writer to express personal and sensory impressions for the enjoyment of the reader.

## 2 Types

- Free verse

## 3 Context

**Subject matter:** response to a selection of questions
**Roles and relationships:** written for readers known or unknown to the writer
**Medium:** books, magazines, Internet, personal diary, poetry reading
**Mode:** written, spoken from written text

## 4 Text

### How to write free verse

**Structure**
- The writer considers a number of focus questions relating to the participants involved in a particular situation and writes the poem in response to these questions.
- no set rhyme scheme
- conversational, rather than poetic, rhythm
- usually fewer words, with more meaning, than prose

**Vocabulary**
- words chosen to focus on and effectively describe the people in the poems and their actions
- use of metaphors and similes, e.g. *Her hair was silk; as sweet as honey*

**Grammar**
- present tense; past tense, e.g. *I am walking; I walked*
- personal pronouns, e.g. *I, we*
- may not be grammatically correct, e.g. no capitals, no sentences, no punctuation

# At night

As the sirens ring through the air

I crawl awkwardly

Down the twisted stairs

Using the flames to light my way

I clutch the small precious bundle close to my chest

Smoke fills the air

Breathing becomes more and more difficult

Loud creaking noises fill me with fear

Doubts cloud my mind

Daylight beckons beyond the wall of flames

I am falling

I hear talking

Rescuing arms reach us in time

Focus questions to ask before writing a poem:

- What time is it?

- Where are you going?

- How are you moving?

- What lights your way?

- What do you have in your pocket?

- What are your thoughts?

- What startles you?

- Describe the smells/sounds of the night.

- Describe the fading of the light and the coming of dawn.

The words of the poem answer the questions.

## 1  Purpose

The purpose is to 'break open' a given poem to develop a deeper understanding of the author's poetic devices that make up the poem in its entirety.

## 2  Types

Poetry analysis can be used on a range of poetry types.

## 3  Context

**Subject matter:** according to the poem being analysed
**Roles and relationships:** The analyst is trying to understand which poetic devices the author employed to create the poem, and how these devices make for a successful reading of the poem.
**Medium:** online, books, newspapers, magazines
**Mode:** written, spoken

## 4  Text

### How to analyse a poem using the SMILES method

**Structure**

- Consider the composition of the poem, i.e. line length, organisation of text, rhyme scheme, syllables, repetition, grammar, e.g. ABABCDCD EFEFGDGD alternate rhyme scheme; two stanzas of eight lines each.

**Meaning**

- Consider the title, overall theme, message and subject. Remember that a poem may have a deeper meaning than it first appears.

**Imagery**

- How does the language of the poem evoke the five senses?
- What literary features have been used? e.g. symbolism, irony. Paterson uses imagery and visual pictures of softness to describe the beauty of the land in the spring, **e.g. *a waving of the grass*** illustrates gentle movement, ***a murmur of myriad bees*** creates a soft sound, ***scent in the blossom*** creates a perfume. This beauty is then contrasted with the harshness of the land during drought in the second stanza, **e.g. *the stock / Tumble down in their tracks, a tottering flock*.**

**Language**

- Poets carefully craft each word of their poems. Consider the use of words – simple, complex, lyrical, colloquial, ironic etc.

- Look at the grammar and punctuation, e.g. the full stops used for the last lines of each stanza.
- Consider the poetic devices used: e.g. anaphora, alliteration, hyperbole, juxtaposition, literal or figurative language, repetition, simile. Paterson uses anaphora at the beginnings of some neighbouring lines – when 'And' is repeated – to emphasise the image: *And a song in the air, / And a murmur of myriad bees, And the breath of the Spring, And Springtime I sing, And the combat I sing*. Anaphora is also used with the word 'There': *There is a waving of grass, There is scent ..., There is drought on the land, and the stock.*

**Effect**

- What is the opinion, bias or message presented by the poet?
- What is the mood of the poem?
- Consider your own reaction to the poem.

**Sound**

- Consider the sound devices used, e.g. onomatopoeia, alliteration, rhythm of spoken text. Paterson uses alliteration in several places, **e.g. *fighting for fate*.** Look also at the last lines of each stanza. The hard 'c' of combat contrasts with the soft 's' of sing to suggest the negative change in fortunes.

# A Singer of the Bush

### Andrew Barton 'Banjo' Paterson

There is a waving of grass in the breeze
And a song in the air,
And a murmur of myriad bees
That toil everywhere.
There is scent in the blossom and bough,
And the breath of the Spring
Is as soft as a kiss on a brow –
And Springtime I sing.

There is drought on the land, and the stock
Tumble down in their tracks
Or follow – a tottering flock –
The scrub-cutter's axe.
While ever a creature survives
The axes shall swing;
We are fighting with fate for their lives –
And the combat I sing.

## 1 Purpose

The purpose of a poster is to present a visual summary of information about a topic or event.

## 2 Types

- Poster
- Chart

## 3 Context

**Subject matter:** wide variety of subjects; can be serious, educational or entertaining and lighthearted
**Roles and relationships:** The author has the knowledge and educates the reader.
**Medium:** single sheets of paper, cardboard, online
**Mode:** written, drawn

## 4 Text

### How to prepare a chart or poster

**Structure**
- Put the information into draft form, i.e. written, visual.
- Decide how the information will be organised, e.g. questions and answers; main heading and subheadings; blocks of information.
- Sequence the information.
- Decide how to record the information, e.g. writing, painting, drawing, computer-generated.
- Decide how to arrange the pictures, maps, labels; there may be more visuals than written text; use of bullet points.
- Size of fonts:
  - title: largest font; should be readable from at least five metres away
  - sub headings: large
  - supporting material: medium
  - details: smallest.

**Vocabulary**
- list of attributes or features of the topic or subject

**Grammar**
- short sentences; complete sentences not always necessary
- phrases and single words
- short paragraphs
- captions
- short headings

# All victims of Cyclone Debbie need your support

## Give Generously

**People in the northern parts of Queensland have had their homes and businesses devastated by this cyclone.
It will take many months to recover. Your help will provide financial and moral support.**

Donations can be made online, or at any branch of the NQBC Bank.

## 1 Purpose

Although Microsoft PowerPoint is a computer program rather than a text type, it is used extensively in the presentation of reports, instructions and descriptions. The purpose of the PowerPoint presentation is to present information or build an argument.

## 2 Types

- Presentations
- Projects
- Explanations
- Reviews

## 3 Context

**Subject matter:** variety of factual/educational subjects
**Roles and relationships:** The author is the authority, who presents information that can be clearly understood by the reader.
**Medium:** computer, using PowerPoint, Google Slides, Prezi or similar
**Mode:** written, spoken

## 4 Text

### How to prepare a PowerPoint presentation

**Structure**
- Preparation: research the content and construct the argument/sequence the information.
- Decide on the slides to be presented.
- Construct the PowerPoint slides.
- Go to 'Slide sorter' to get an overview of the presentation.
- Delete and edit as necessary.
- Use pictures and animations to complement the presentation.
- Practise delivering the presentation.
- The presentation should not be read from the screen.

**Vocabulary**
- Include an introduction with a relevant and catchy title.
- Use bullet points on each slide.
- Each bullet point should contain only a few words or short phrases which outline the key points of the presentation.
- Factual language is used to build an argument.

**Grammar**
- short phrases
- single words

## PowerPoint Tips

Eight steps to an engaging presentation

## Content First, Technology Second  1

First: prepare content, e.g. an argument

Second: 'bells and whistles'

## Tell A Story  2

Story may be:
- a narrative
- an argument
- an information report

Steps:
- Draw a storyboard on paper
- Construct the PowerPoint presentation
- View, sort, add, delete or edit slides

## Effective Written Text  3

- Introduction, including a relevant and catchy title
- Short bullet points, i.e. use only a few words or short phrases

## Use Visual Metaphors  4

Visuals:
- are a powerful way to tell your story
- help the content be understood
- include cartoons, graphs, icons and symbols
- help to avoid an overuse of written text

## Using Animation Effectively  5

Animation:
- adds to the spectacle
- helps to tell the story
- helps to add new information
- can hide information that is yet to come

## Visual Clarity and Impact  6

- Ensure a good contrast between:
  - the background colour of the slides
  - the colour of the text
  - the colours of the visuals
- Avoid dark text on a dark background
- Ask a friend for feedback on presentation

## Presentation  7

- Construction of the slides is the first part of the preparation
- Presenting your information or argument is the second part
- Spend time preparing the delivery of the presentation

## Delivery  8

- Communicate: the way you speak should relate to the text
- Body and spoken language both important
- Essential elements for speakers:
  - eye contact with the audience
  - clear and audible pronunciation
  - a fluent and relaxed speaking style
- Don't read from the screen

1  Content First, Technology Second
2  Tell A Story
3  Use Written Text Effectively
4  Use Visual Metaphors
5  Using Animation Effectively
6  Visual Clarity and Impact
7  Presentation
8  Delivery

Summary

## 1  Purpose

The purpose of a procedure is to inform or direct someone about how to do something.

## 2  Types

- Recipes
- Directions
- Rules
- Instructions
- Science experiments

## 3  Context

**Subject matter:** related to giving advice on how to make or do something, e.g. cooking, map reading, building projects
**Roles and relationships:** The writer has the knowledge and is advising known or unknown readers.
**Medium:** recipe book, instruction manual, brochures, science books, cooking/home renovation programs on TV
**Mode:** written, spoken

## 4  Text

How to write the procedure, e.g. a recipe or a science experiment
**Structure**
- title of the recipe or experiment
- list of ingredients or materials
- series of steps, written in order, so that the recipe or experiment is carried out correctly
- diagrams and illustrations that are used to make the text clearer

**Vocabulary**
- specialised vocabulary related to the topic, **e.g. *sift the flour and salt together*; *combine the chemicals***
- impersonal language; do not use *I* or *you*

**Grammar**
- short sentences beginning with a command
- action verbs used to give commands/instructions, **e.g. *beat, add, sift, bake***
- steps, numbered and put in the correct sequence

# Patty cakes

Title of the recipe or aim of the experiment

## Ingredients

3 tablespoons butter
½ cup sugar
1 egg
¼ teaspoon vanilla
1 cup self-raising flour
pinch salt
¼ cup milk

List of ingredients or materials

## Method

1   Preheat oven to 180°C.
2   Beat butter and sugar to a cream.
3   Add lightly beaten egg and vanilla. Beat well.
4   Stir flour and salt together.
5   Fold in dry ingredients alternately with milk and mix well.
6   Drop heaped teaspoonfuls of mixture into well-greased patty tins or papers.
7   Bake for 10 to 15 minutes.
8   Cool on a wire rack.
9   Ice with butter icing (optional).

Short sentences beginning with a command verb. Steps are in sequence and are numbered.

## Servings

Makes about 12.

Results are written.

## 1 Purpose

The purpose of the recount is to inform or entertain by retelling past events or experiences.

## 2 Types

- Personal
- Factual

## 3 Context

**Subject matter:** focus on a specific person, place or event
**Roles and relationships:** The writer may or may not know the readers.
**Medium:** journal, recount of excursion, letters and diaries, anecdote
**Mode:** written, spoken

## 4 Text

### How to write a recount

**Structure**

- Orientation: the writer informs the reader of the details concerning the who, what, when and where of the event or situation.
- events:
  - arranged in order
  - each point relating to one particular event
  - comments may express the writer's feelings or impressions about the situation
  - reorientation – may conclude with a personal comment

**Vocabulary**

- personal, emotive and descriptive words may be used
- personal, e.g. *I, we*
- emotive, e.g. *I felt more worried ...*
- descriptive, e.g. *a bulky item wrapped in a blanket*
- time expressions important, e.g. *At 11 o'clock ...*

**Grammar**

- action verbs, e.g. *forced, disappeared, gave chase, tackled*
- usually written in the past tense, e.g. *As I approached ...*
- cause and effect structures, e.g. *Fearing that he would escape ...*

# Police witness statement · · · · · · · · · · **Title**

At about 11 o'clock on the night of 29 July 2017, I was walking down
Stafford Road from the bus stop, on my way home from the city.
There were a few cars passing down the road, but no pedestrians.

**Orientation**
The introduction contains
precise details

I was walking eastwards on the left-hand side of the street when I
heard a noise. A dark figure was trying to force open the front door
of a house on the other side of the street. He had something in his
hand, a jemmy or similar tool. I could see that he was trying to lever
the door to get inside.

Recount develops in
chronological order

As I approached, hiding behind a bush near the fence, I heard him
muttering under his breath. I looked closely at the house. Number
163 is on the corner of Stafford and Mary streets. There were no
lights on and the house had a deserted feel, as if no one was home, or
maybe the residents were on holidays. No one else seemed to have
noticed the man or the noise he was making. There were no lights in
the apartments of the multistorey building next door.

Detailed step-by-step
description

Standing behind the bush, I saw the door give way and the man
had disappeared inside. At this point, I felt more worried for any
residents inside than I did for my own safety. I called 000 and spoke
to someone at Police Headquarters. He assured me that the Stafford
Police Station was just around the corner. The local police would be
there within five minutes. 'Don't take any risks,' he warned me.

Reference to personal
feelings

Use of dialogue creates
authenticity and realism

I promised to heed his advice, but as I hung up, the man emerged
from the house, carrying a bulky item wrapped in a blanket. Fearing
that he would escape into a nearby vehicle, I gave chase along the
footpath and tackled him. As we both landed on the grass verge, he
lost his grip on the stolen item, a large oriental vase, which shattered
onto the footpath.

Detailed account of
action

Just as the man was reaching for his jemmy to attack me, the police
arrived and disarmed him.

I was taken to the station along with the man under arrest and asked
to complete this statement.

Reorientation

Roberto Ricardo

## 1 Purpose

The purpose of a book review is to evaluate a text. A book review allows the writer to draw attention to, and make judgements about, the features, strengths and weaknesses of a book, and to voice his or her opinion of it.

## 2 Types

- **Book review:** a review of a fiction or nonfiction book
- **Literature review:** an examination and review of a range of academic sources

## 3 Context

**Subject matter:** any subject, e.g. could be any fiction or nonfiction book
**Roles and relationships:** The writer presents a critique of the text to known/unknown readers for discussion.
**Medium:** assignments, newspapers, magazines, speeches
**Mode:** written, spoken

## 4 Text

### How to write a book review

**Structure**

1 A brief introduction containing:
   - title, author and publishing information
   - setting
   - main characters
   - problem/conflict (briefly).
2 Reviewer's opinions should be a main part of the review and should discuss:
   - strengths and weaknesses of the book
   - theme/message, i.e. *What is the argument or conflict?* and *Is it resolved?* It is important to understand the argument or conflict within the story in order to discuss whether or not the author has created a situation that justified or resolved the issue at hand.
   - author's writing style, e.g. *Does the author communicate a clear message or theme? Would you read another book by this author? How does this book compare with other books that you have read by this author?*
- A good reviewer:
   - makes notes about the book in a graphic organiser as the text is read
   - backs up opinions with facts or examples, or other supporting evidence in the form of direct or indirect quotes from the book

gives due credit to the author for quotations by using quotation marks and/or reference to the author and page number of the book.

3 The conclusion should:
   - restate the reviewer's opinion – consistent, clear and direct reasons for liking the book or not
   - tie the opinions back into the summary
   - give others a point of discussion
   - be brief.

**Vocabulary**
- evaluative language
- persuasive language to express and justify an opinion
- specialised vocabulary necessary, e.g. to discuss poetic techniques like imagery

**Grammar**
- topic sentences
- variety of sentence structures, e.g. compound and complex sentences, expanded clauses
- connectives to link paragraphs and subjects/ideas
- evidence of editing
- accurate spelling and punctuation

# Book review: *A Waltz for Matilda*

*A Waltz for Matilda*, written by Jackie French and published in 2010, is set in the period from the late 1800s through to the early 1900s, after federation. The story concerns a young woman growing up in this significant time in Australia's history. The underlying theme is working together and never giving up. 'The things he fought for will live forever … We stand together … and forge a new nation.'

This era is a time of turmoil with many issues like racism and inequality affecting ordinary people. Australian states are not united, and women and Indigenous people are not allowed to vote. Droughts, strikes, wars, union campaigns for federation and new laws form the background of this story.

Matilda is born in this era. Her family is very poor and her mother is extremely ill. After she dies, Matilda at the age of 12 makes the decision to search for her father, a stockman living in the country. She has never met him but has heard about him from her mother. However, when she finds him, he is a swaggie wanted by the troopers, '… not tall and handsome like her mother has described'.

Nevertheless, father and daughter are able to establish a good relationship. The times are difficult but Matilda quickly learns to love the land, 'the gold bones of the landscape … it was hard beauty but real'. The visual images of the text paint pictures of the country in drought for the reader; flood and good times and the consequences of these times are made clear.

When Matilda runs away with her father to a billabong, we are introduced to the song *Waltzing Matilda*. At the time, the troopers are trying to capture Matilda's father for stealing a sheep. Thus the song has significance for him and for the union men, as it is a song about courage and symbolises the spirit of a new nation where men and women want the right to have a say about their lives.

Matilda continues to survive against all odds in this harsh and brutal land. Conflicts arise with a wealthy landowner and the shearers who don't like to take instructions from a young woman. She shows us her strength of character and ability to learn to deal with diverse groups of people. These strengths contribute to the building of her character and help her to become an independent woman.

The language of the book is beautifully descriptive. The author's use of personification in 'The fire's voice was lower, higher, a sound with no name'; and the effective use of Australian expressions like 'who the flaming hell are you,' and the idiom 'send her down Hughie' all add to the novel's Australian flavour.

The author cleverly weaves the story of the struggles of a determined young girl, Matilda, into the history of a time of great change in Australia. The strength of the book lies in the variety of characters who give us a clear picture of all those involved in the fight to make the country a better and fairer place in which to live.

**Introduction:**
- sets the scene
- describes the historical background of the book
- summarises theme
- introduces main character/s

**Details the main events of the novel:**
- death of her mother
- life with her father
- significance of unions
- life on her own

Conflicts, resolutions

Language discussed, e.g. personification, idioms

Conclusion evaluates the story from the perspective of Australia's history and as a piece of fiction

## 1  Purpose

The purpose of the review is to inform and persuade.

## 2  Types

- Print media
- Electronic media

## 3  Context

**Subject matter:** focus is on a play script
**Roles and relationships:** The writer is a drama critic.
**Medium:** newspaper, online publication, radio program
**Mode:** written, spoken

## 4  Text

### How to write a review of a play

**Structure**

- a combination of title, author and director; main actors
- details of theatre, time, dates and cost of performance
- needs an angle/general opinionative comment, **e.g. *Another Willy Russell classic***
- brief plot analysis and speculation on the ending of the play
- ending not revealed
- analysis of key aspects of the play in a paragraph for each
- key narrative techniques include: theme or issue, plot, genre, characters, setting

**Vocabulary**

- formal
- literary language/the language of dramatic performance
- informative and opinionative, **e.g. *This creates humour, which balances well ...***
- impersonal language is the safe option, **e.g. *The tragic ending leaves the audience ...***

**Grammar**

- correct English
- sentence fragments used for emphasis
- first person acceptable in moderation, but not necessary
- second person, addressing the reader, acceptable but not necessary
- present tense

# Blood Brothers

by Willy Russell
Directed by John Dayton
Caxton Theatre
20 June – 5 July

Practical information
about the production

## *More bloody than brotherly*

Catchy headline
uses alliteration to
summarise the play

Another Willy Russell classic is coming to the Caxton. Following on the success of *Educating Rita*, this is Russell's most famous play, a musical drama. Twins Mickey and Eddie are separated at birth as Mickey's mother, Mrs Johnson, cannot afford to bring up two more children. Persuaded by her rich but childless employer, she reluctantly parts with Edward, but the two boys are brought up in the same town. Inevitably, they meet as teenagers and this is where the trouble begins.

Background about the
playwright/general plot
outline but withholding
the ending

While not a very original basis for a plot, the play does develop in an interesting way, ending very dramatically. Both boys are very much a product of their environment. Mickey (Sean Jackson) is streetwise and a natural leader, whereas Edward (David Hamilton) is a naive and spoilt only child. Naturally, they both fall for the same girl, Linda (Natalie Parsons).

Opinionative topic
sentence opens the
paragraph/insight into
character

What makes this production particularly appealing in Act 1, especially, is the use of the adult actors dressed as children in oversized clothing, with smuts on their faces and dirt on their clothes. This creates humour, which balances well with the later seriousness of the plot. The actors are competent in their roles, with standout performances by the charismatic Mickey, who is idolised by his weaker twin, and by Eve Douglas as Mrs Lyons, Edward's 'mother', with her superior manner and irritating social graces.

Opinionative topic
sentence/evaluation of
the actors

The set is minimalist, but this suits the genre of the musical drama very well. The audience will enjoy the music as well as the drama, as all the actors have been selected for their vocal as well as their acting talents. The issues of social class and nature versus nurture emerge in the play, as well as a warning about deception and taking the law into your own hands. The tragic ending leaves the audience with much to think about. Another triumph for director John Dayton.

Opinionative topic
sentence/general
conclusion about
issues/final sentences
encourage readers to
see the play

*Julie Turner*

## 1 Purpose

The purpose of a feature film script is to entertain.

## 2 Types

- Comedy
- Drama
- Action

## 3 Context

**Subject matter:** a fictional narrative
**Roles and relationships:** The scriptwriter is writing for an unknown audience.
**Medium:** written script for production into a film – visual medium
**Mode:** written

## 4 Text

### How to write a film script

**Structure**
- narrative structure: orientation, complication, resolution
- written in scenes featuring characters and setting

**Vocabulary**
- detailed narrative so that producer/director can visualise action and mood
- dialogue appropriate to characters and context, **e.g. *LOU: C'mon ...***
- stage directions to indicate movement and mood, **e.g. *(gesturing for him to follow)***
- uses film language related to camerawork, **e.g. *AERIAL SHOT PANS***

**Grammar**
- formal grammar in the film script
- emphasis on realism in dialogue, rather than grammatical correctness
- use of sentence fragments, **e.g. *Probably just rubbish someone's dumped.***
- spoken language may include dialects and colloquialisms

# *Finders Keepers*

FADE IN: EXT. PARK. DAY.

AERIAL SHOT PANS across tall trees to a small area where colourful
playground equipment has been recently installed. SILENCE, AS
CAMERA HOVERS then ZOOMS into the playground. Two
children are playing on a climbing frame, a girl about 10 years
old and a smaller boy. Both are wearing dark-coloured shorts and
T-shirts. Their feet are bare. Faint sounds of traffic, growing louder.

Script uses formal language

Script is descriptive to aid in film-making

CUT TO: TRAFFIC SHOT – PEAK HOUR, AND BACK TO
THE PARK.

Climbing easily to the top of the metal frame that resembles the
bones of a dinosaur, the girl watches the boy struggling to reach her.
A HIGH ANGLE SHOT follows the boy's progress.

Camera directions are precise

LOU: C'mon. (gesturing for him to follow) You can do it, Sammy.
Good boy! (nodding and smiling)

CLOSE-UP OF GIRL watching intently as he takes hold of the
rope ladder and hauls himself up. She crawls down the backbone of
the dinosaur onto its tail and then jumps across to a nearby elevated
platform. Sammy follows her. There is a thumping sound as he lands
safely beside her.

Script includes detailed direction on sound, movement and facial expression

LOU: Good view! (standing, shading her eyes against the sunlight)

The CAMERA follows her eye as she scans the skyline. But Sammy
is not interested in the view. He pulls on the bottom of her T-shirt to
get her attention.

SAMMY: (pointing to something in the distance) What's that?

Lou squints and looks across to a clump of trees, the CAMERA
TILTING to follow her gaze. Under a tree sits a small cardboard box.

Script is in narrative form, structured in scenes

SAMMY: Maybe it's treasure. (climbing down the metal ladder that
leads from the platform to the ground)

Lou follows, the CAMERA PANNING between them as Sammy
runs towards the mysterious box.

SAMMY: (holds up his hand as a warning) Look, it's moving. Maybe
there's a snake inside.

LOU: (leaning forward to open the lid) Maybe it's a kitten.

CLOSE-UP OF THEIR FACES AS CAMERA PANS BETWEEN
THE CHILDREN AND FINALLY TILTS TO THE CONTENTS
OF THE BOX.

Narrative builds to a climax, with suspense

SAMMY: (eyes wide with wonder) It's a baby, Lou. A tiny baby.

## 1 Purpose

The purpose of a play script is to entertain.

## 2 Types

- Comedy
- Tragedy
- History
- Drama/crime

## 3 Context

**Subject matter:** a narrative with plot and characters
**Roles and relationships:** written for an unknown audience
**Medium:** live performance, stage performance
**Mode:** spoken delivery from a written script

## 4 Text

### How to write a play script

**Structure**

- play script divided into scenes and acts
- written in dialogue, e.g. *What ... are you doing here?*
- stage directions to describe movement, gesture, facial expression and interaction between characters, e.g. *(rubbing her eyes sleepily)*
- plot involves conflict between and/or within characters, e.g. *Help you? I'm taking you home right now!*
- number of characters and setting restricted by stage performance

**Vocabulary**

- dialogue to suit the social and cultural context of the play as well as the characters' ages, genders, personalities, plus the social and historical setting/social and cultural context of the play
- language may include colloquialisms, slang, e.g. *You wanna get me into trouble?*

**Grammar**

- sentence fragments; emphasis on realism rather than grammatical correctness
- all tenses can be used
- first, second or third person

# The Stowaway

## Scene 3: An isolated rural property in the hinterland

In trouble with her mother, ANGIE has decided to run away from home. The perfect opportunity comes when she sees the van belonging to a fisherman she and her brother have been talking to on the beach. She slides the side door open and climbs in, hiding herself under a blanket. Minutes later, unaware of her presence, the man climbs into the driver's seat and heads for his home in the nearby hills.

FRANK: *(sliding the door of his van open, noting a lump underneath the blanket)* What's this? *(He pulls the blanket off)* What ... are you doing here?

ANGIE: *(rubbing her eyes sleepily)* Hello. Where am I?

FRANK: *(angrily)* Never mind that. What are you doing in my van? And where's your brother?

ANGIE: *(looking up at him)* Felix is gone. *(She bursts into tears.)*

FRANK: Gone. You mean gone home, like you should have done. Not hidden in my van. You wanna get me into trouble?

ANGIE: *(thoughtfully, drying her eyes)* No, mister, but you have to help me.

FRANK: *(glaring at her)* Help you? I'm taking you home right now!

ANGIE: *(terrified)* No! My mother'll kill me! Oh, please, mister. *(Then defiantly)* I won't tell you my address.

FRANK: The police station then. Come on. Let's go!

ANGIE: No! You have to help me! You have to!

FRANK: Why should I help you? You're a stowaway. Get in the front. And put your seat belt on. *(He begins to close the side door of the van.)*

ANGIE: *(desperately)* No, wait! Not the police! Take me to my dad's house. Please ...

FRANK: Where does he live?

ANGIE: Sydney.

FRANK: Sydney? That's over a thousand kilometres away. Are you mad? Why should I take you there?

ANGIE: *(slowly, looking at him seriously)* Because if you don't take me to Sydney, I'll tell the police you kidnapped me ... and Felix.

FRANK: Felix! Where is Felix?

ANGIE: I don't know. I think he's lost.

FRANK: *(burying his face in his hands)* He's not the only one.

---

Title gives a clue to the plot

Setting is described in the script

Background information: the story so far

Stage directions indicate movement

Speeches are usually short interchanges

Stage directions indicate mood

Dialogue creates atmosphere and suspense / vocabulary establishes character / language suits the situation

Conflict develops as the scene progresses

Character traits emerge as the plot develops

Simple everyday language forms a realistic interchange between characters/informal spoken language is used in drama

Angie's character becomes calculating and threatening

Scene ends on a note of tension and suspense

## 1  Purpose

The purpose of a survey is to collect information.

## 2  Types

- Multiple-choice
- Short answers

## 3  Context

**Subject matter:** questions designed to collect information on a specific topic; surveys are done on a variety of topics, e.g. shopping choices, fitness levels
**Roles and relationships:** The writer and the readers may be known or unknown to each other.
**Medium:** magazine, phone call, Internet, face to face
**Mode:** written, spoken from a written text

## 4  Text

### How to write a survey

**Structure**

- Brainstorm what you want to find out and the questions you will need to ask to find out this information.
- Write down the questions in sentences.
- Put questions in order.
- Questions should range from the simplest to the more difficult.
- Using open-ended questions beginning with *How* or *Why* will give you more information than yes/no questions beginning with *Do you, Are you, Have you* etc.
- Write a summary of your results and discuss your findings.
- A survey sheet should:
  - be easily read, understood and answered
  - provide spaces for responses.

**Vocabulary**

- Use words that are:
  - clear and concise
  - suitable for the age, knowledge and understanding of the reader.

**Grammar**

- Readers must be able to read and answer questions quickly so questions must be written in simple sentences.

# Survey on daily exercise

Target group: _____

Date: _____

Number surveyed: _____

1   What age group do you fit into?
- ☐ 10–15 years
- ☐ 16–20 years
- ☐ 21–30 years
- ☐ 31–40 years
- ☐ 41–50 years
- ☐ 50+ years

2   Do you exercise every day?
- ☐ Yes*
- ☐ No

If your answer is Yes, how do you exercise?

_____
_____
_____

\* If you answered Yes, go to Question 4.

3   How many times a week do you exercise?
- ☐ None
- ☐ 1–2
- ☐ 3–5
- ☐ More than 5

4   Do you enjoy exercise?
- ☐ Yes
- ☐ No

5   How do you exercise?
- ☐ Alone
- ☐ Partner
- ☐ Group

6   When you exercise, what form of activity do you undertake?
- ☐ Walking
- ☐ Jogging
- ☐ Swimming
- ☐ Gym
- ☐ Gardening
- ☐ Playing sport

Other:

_____
_____
_____

7   Where do you exercise?
- ☐ At a gym
- ☐ At home
- ☐ On an oval

Other places:

_____
_____
_____

8   How would you classify your fitness at the moment?
- ☐ Poor
- ☐ Fair
- ☐ Average
- ☐ Above average
- ☐ Excellent

## 1 Purpose

Twitter is an online social networking service that enables its users to send and read text-based posts, of maximum length 280 characters (recently increased from 140), known as 'tweets'.

## 2 Types

- Twitter for teachers
  - networking and collaborating with teachers, school districts or teacher resource groups to share ideas and information
  - requesting information, assistance, e.g. recommended books, lesson ideas, teaching tools
- Twitter for parents
  - requesting information from, or sharing information with, the school/individual teachers
- Twitter for students
  - developing a story, e.g. teacher chooses a genre for a story, tweets an opening and asks students to contribute to the story
  - collaborating to edit all the tweets into a coherent story
  - contributing to a discussion, e.g. students produce a dialogue between two opposing characters
  - completing word play activities, e.g. anagrams: post eight letters and see how many new words students can create
  - teacher posts a word and students post synonyms, antonyms, homonyms; creates a 'wordle' of responses

## 3 Pros and cons

### Pros for students

Twitter:
- is free for everyone
- is an online record of ideas discussed in class (for assessment)
- can empower students.

### Pros for teachers

Twitter is:
- a great self-reflection tool
- a time-efficient way to stay up-to-date on the latest education trends, news and research
- a great way to participate in professional development.

### Cons

- It can be very time-consuming to set up and manage a class set of Twitter accounts.
- Cyber-vandalism can be a serious problem.
- twitter.com may be blocked by the school/education authority.

# Questions posed for new state representative after an election

As of Monday 25 March, local member John Smith replied to questions posed via Twitter by Brisbane students.

**@Newzone12 to @JohnSmith**
What are your plans for your new cabinet in the first 3 months?

**@JohnSmith to @Newzone12**
Cabinet meets this week to prioritise actions for the first three months. We plan to implement the promises that won over so many Queenslanders.

**@Newzone12 to @JohnSmith**
Can you be more specific?

**@JohnSmith to @Newzone12**
Action on water, electricity and car registration costs to ease the burden on voters.

Twitter allows for responses of no more than 280 characters so the replies are short

## 1  Purpose

Wikis are websites that allow for the creation of different web pages by numerous users who collaborate and cooperate to produce a new product.

## 2  Types

Wikis can be used:
- by individuals learning to contribute to and edit group work
- by students and teachers to write, plan and cooperate together
- as focal points for class discussions
- to draft collaborative documents such as leadership policies, simulated government legislation or haiku poetry
- to write peer reviews
- to brainstorm ideas for group research and make notes, e.g. mind mapping
- as a source of feedback
- to comment or to monitor the progress and level of student contributions
- to collaborate in the creation of a class project, e.g. divide class into small groups; each small group writes about a specific article in their own wiki; wikis combined as a whole class project.

## 3  Context

**Subject matter:** variety of imaginative, creative, factual or educational subjects
**Roles and relationships:** The writer contributes to a collaborative text or evaluates individual progress; the audience may be known or unknown, but a wiki usually operates within a defined private community.
**Medium:** Internet
**Mode:** written
**Setting up:**
- A classroom wiki project needs to be set up through the school's technology department.
- A personal wiki could be set up through Wikimedia.

## 4  Text

Structure, grammar and vocabulary will vary according to the type of genre used, e.g. if a poem is to be written, students could follow suggestions in the poetry section.
Wikis can be a bit chaotic. The skills of negotiation need to be addressed to help resolve disagreements over editing that can occur.

**HOME** | **DISCUSSIONS** | **PHOTOS** | **NEWS** | **VIDEOS** | **UPDATES** | **MEMBERS**

# WHAT ARE THE PROBLEMS FOR OUR ENVIRONMENT?

Email us or join our discussions

## Home

Global warming is a big issue that we are facing at this moment. Many scientists believe that if we don't acknowledge that there is a problem we could face serious problems with the environment in the future. They suggest that global warming or the overheating of the atmosphere will cause many changes. Today many areas are experiencing significant differences in their seasonal weather patterns which have resulted in either droughts or floods.

There have been floods in many countries. In recent years in Australia flooding has become a big issue. Many people have lost their houses and livelihoods. Crops were destroyed and this has seriously affected the economy.

Watch the video *Fight for the Planet* to learn about the impact humans have on the environment and what needs to be done to reverse global warming.

## Glossary

**active verb:** verb used when the subject is the doer of an action, e.g. *The boy **patted** the dog.*

**alliteration:** the repetition of consonant sounds, especially in poetry

**anaphora:** intentional repetition of a word or phrase at the beginning of several sentences or paragraphs

**chronological:** according to time sequence, in order

**classifying language:** expressions that put a person or event in the context of time, place and group, e.g. *He was one of the best known Australian writers of the 20th century.*

**climax:** a turning point, the height of a crisis

**colloquial:** used in ordinary or familiar conversation; not formal or literary

**context:** important background or circumstances relating to a text, including who is writing it, who will read it, the subject matter, how the text is structured and how it is delivered to the audience

**figurative language:** makes comparisons, uses words for dramatic or poetic effect; opposite of literal language

**genre:** a specific text type, e.g. fantasy or crime fiction

**hyperbole:** exaggerated statements or claims not intended to be taken literally

**hypothesis:** a thesis or contention, point of view or angle that is proved in an essay or in writing

**idiom:** a form of expression peculiar to a language, especially one having a significance other than its literal one

**imagery:** visual language, often figurative language, used in literary texts

**imperative:** a command or strong advice

**irony/ironic:** a gap between what is said and what is meant, like sarcasm

**juxtaposition:** the fact of two things being seen or placed close together with contrasting effect

**literal language:** words are used exactly according to their meaning; free from exaggeration or distortion

**medium:** the channel of delivery of a message, e.g. radio, newspaper, book

**metaphor:** a form of figurative language that compares two objects by saying that one is the other

**mode:** the method used to deliver a message, e.g. spoken, written

**orientation:** the introduction; setting the scene for the message

**passive verb:** verb used when the subject is the receiver of an action, e.g. *The dog **was patted** by the boy.*

**person:** (in grammar) shows the relationship between a subject and a verb:

- **first person** – the person speaking, e.g. *I/we*
- **second person** – the person listening or being spoken to, e.g. *you*
- **third person** – the person being spoken about, e.g. *he/she/they*

**personification:** to give human qualities to things or animals

**purpose:** the reason for writing the text

**relationships:** a statement relating to whether the reader and writer are known to each other or not

**reorientation:** restating the original aim or direction of a text

**roles:** a statement relating to the function of the writer and reader, e.g. writer educates; reader learns

**sequencing:** putting items/lists/events into a logical order

**simile:** comparing two objects using the words 'like' or 'as'

**structure:** the way the text is put together

**tense:** the form of a verb indicating when an action happened, i.e. past, present, future, e.g. *he* **eats**; *he* **ate**; *he* **will eat**

**text:** the writing

**voice:** the form of the verb in the sentence that indicates if the action is being caused by the subject or happening to the subject:

- **active voice:** the subject is causing the action, e.g. *The dog* **bit** *the boy.*
- **passive voice:** the action is happening to the subject, e.g. *The boy* **was bitten** *by the dog.*

# Writing activities

1  **Advertisement:** Create an advertisement for teachers and parents about the advantages – or disadvantages – of homework.

2  **Biography:** Interview a grandparent, aunt, uncle or other older person. Write their biography.

3  **Blog:** Write a blog about your favourite food. Include historical and other facts.

4  **Brochure/flyer:** Your school is raising money for a local charity. Create a brochure/flyer to persuade the community to contribute. The brochure will be distributed by letterbox drop.

5  **Debate:** In pairs, one takes the affirmative side while the other takes the negative side. The topic is: 'Co-educational schools are better.'

6  **Description:** Write a description of your bedroom.

7  **Email:** Prepare and send an email to your teacher to thank them for teaching you.

8  **Essay:** Write a persuasive essay about whether Australia should host the next Olympic Games or not.

9  **Editorial:** Create a persuasive editorial about lowering the voting age to 16.

10  **Explanation:** Write an explanation of an iPhone for someone who has never seen one before and is unaware of its uses.

11  **Information report:** Prepare an information report about your school, for someone who is considering enrolling.

12  **Infographic:** Using either Canva or another online application, create an infographic about the benefits of eating fruit.

13  **Interview:** In pairs, interview your partner about their best and worst school experiences. Cover all '5W + H' (what, when, why, who, where and how) aspects of these experiences.

14  **Letter:** Write a letter to your local member of parliament to state your opinion about public transport in your area. Consider all aspects, including cost, timetables, reliability and convenience.

15  **Narrative:** Compose your own narrative about 'getting lost'.

16  **News article:** Create a news article about an upcoming event.

17  **Novel:** Compose a plot capsule or summary of a novel. Use your imagination or base your summary on a film you have viewed or an online game you've played.

18  **Novel: essay:** Discuss the central character in a novel you have read and how they develop in the text.

19  **Podcast:** Prepare a podcast for older listeners about playing online games. Explain how playing games online is the same as, and different from, playing physical games. A Venn diagram will help you arrange your ideas.

20  **Poetry: cinquain, haiku and limerick:** Choose one of these styles, and write a poem about your favourite landscape.

21  **Poetry: free verse:** Write a free verse poem about a hobby of yours.

22  **Poetry: analysis:** Use the SMILES method to analyse Banjo Paterson's 'A Singer of the Bush'. Use the examples provided to help with your analysis.

23  **Poster:** Create a poster that showcases the most popular bands among your friends.

24  **PowerPoint presentation:** Make a PowerPoint presentation about the tallest structures in the world.

25  **Procedure:** Write a procedure for making breakfast. You choose the elements, e.g. a poached egg and toast.

26  **Recount:** Script a recount of a day that was special or different in some way.

27  **Review: book:** Prepare a book review about the novel you are currently reading.

28  **Review: play:** Write a review of a play you have seen or studied.

29  **Script: film:** Create a short film script (with stage directions) about finding something unusual or unexpected.

30  **Script: play:** Write a short play about a conflict with a friend or sibling.